Make the Choice to

Rejoice

No Matter What

David R. Stokes

MAKE THE CHOICE TO REJOICE: No Matter What
Copyright © 2018 David R. Stokes

All rights reserved. No part of this publication may be reproduced, distributed or transmitted in any form or by any means, including photocopying, recording, or other electronic or mechanical methods, without the prior written permission of the publisher, except in the case of brief quotations embodied in critical reviews and certain other noncommercial uses permitted by copyright law.

Expectation Books
Fairfax, Virginia
www.expectationbooks.com

ISBN: 1-947153-05-6
ISBN-13: 978-1-947153-05-9

All scripture references in this book, unless otherwise indicated, are from the New International Version (copyright © 1973, 1978, 1984 by International Bible Society). When other translations are cited, the following initials are used: KJV (King James Version), NKJV (New King James Version), and NLT (New Living Translation).

Cover Design: Eowyn Riggins
Layout: Rachel Greene
Visit the author's website: www.davidrstokes.com

Special discounts are available on quantity purchases by churches and group ministries. For details visit: www.expectationbooks.com.

*For my only granddaughter Karen JOY Vaughan.
Joy is not just her middle name, it's her essence and effect.*

FOREWORD

I know what makes me happy—a good book, a cup of tea in a proper cup and saucer, a WW II documentary on *Netflix*, a day spent with family, cheese, cheese, and more cheese.

But, this isn't a book about happiness. It's a book about joy.

When I stopped to think about what makes me joyful, I was caught off guard. You see, joy and happiness are two very different things.

Happiness is based on what's happening *around* me. Joy is about what's happening *within* me. My happiness is based on circumstances and my emotional response, while joy is based on God's promises and what I know to be true. Mind you, they aren't mutually exclusive—you can have joy and feel happiness, but there's no way to be truly happy without joy.

Look at it this way, how many times have you woken up and thought, "It's going to be a great day!"—but it's all downhill from there? The barista messes up your order, you hit every red light on the way to work, you spill coffee on your white shirt and, by the way, Barbara in HR wants to talk to you.

To paraphrase Julie Andrews, these are not a "few of my favorite things."

But, James tells us to *"Consider it pure joy, my brothers and sisters, whenever you face trials of many kinds."* (James 1:2) What? Joy? Seriously? I have several emotions in these situations, but I can promise you, joy is rarely at the top of the list, if it makes it all

That's because our joy is based on the *results* of our trials, not the trials themselves.

Being joyful in these moments is courageous. It means we're intentionally stepping away from our natural, human response and *making a choice to rejoice* because we can see beyond our circumstances.

As with so many things in life, it's all about our perspective. When we take our eyes off ourselves to consider what God has done for us, responding with thanksgiving and joy becomes a natural response.

That's because our joy is ultimately rooted in the finished work of Christ. Focusing on temporary hardships or current circumstances means our happiness will be brief. If we want joy that remains, we must focus on God's promises.

"And the ransomed of the LORD shall return and come to Zion with singing; everlasting joy shall be upon their heads; they shall obtain gladness and joy, and sorrow and sighing shall flee away." (Isaiah 35:10)

Tracey Dowdy
Editorial Assistant to Pastor David R. Stokes
Expectation Church
Fairfax, Virginia
Expectationbooks.com
April 2018

CHAPTER ONE

A Powerful Choice

Joy and happiness are not the same things.

Ponder that for a moment.

They are certainly related to each other—at least some of the time—but they are not the same. They both involve our emotions, but they are not purely emotional. Understanding the distinction between joy and happiness is crucial to experiencing and appreciating both in greater measure.

My late father-in-law tended to repeat himself—especially as he got older. It was part of his charm. His name was Bob. As I get older, and some in my life who *say* they love me tell me that I'm starting to repeat myself, I find myself remembering the old man even more fondly. Often Bob used wit as a vehicle for wisdom. For example, when someone would say they weren't happy, he would simply ask, "What's Happy?"

Great question.

Blaise Pascal, a seventeenth-century French physicist, mathematician, inventor, and outspoken Christian wrote: "All men seek happiness. This is without exception. Whatever different means they employ, they all tend to this end. The cause of some going to war, and of others avoiding it, is the same desire in both, attended with different views. The will never takes the least step but to this object. This is the motive of every action of every man, even of those who hang themselves."[1]

The word "happy" is rooted in the single syllable "hap," as in *hap*pening or *hap*penstance. It's a very simple concept. Happiness is directly connected to something that has happened, is happening, or might happen. It's a by-product. If you chase it directly, you'll never catch it. But if you chase something else worthwhile, you may just find some happiness nearby.

When I grew up, we didn't have "Wi-Fi" in our home—but we did have "hi-fi."[2] My mom loved to play music on a contraption labeled as "high-fidelity" when she did housework. I got to listen to cutting-edge groups like *Peter, Paul, and Mary*, *The Kingston Trio*, and a particularly mellow cadre of vocalists called *The Ray Conniff Singers*.

So cool.

They had one song my mother especially loved. It was called *Happiness Is*. It had several verses with snappy lyrics like:

---

[1] http://www.ccel.org/ccel/pascal/pensees.toc.html article 425.

[2] Google it. :)

*"To the preacher,
It's a prayer, prayer, prayer.
To the Beatles,
It's a "Yeah, Yeah, Yeah."
To the golfer,
It's a hole in one.
To the father,
It's a brand-new son."*

Then came the unrelenting chorus. It was cool because, in an exercise involving great musical dexterity, half the singers would sing, then the other half would repeat. It was like the *Cirque du Soleil* of choral music.

*"Happiness is
(Happiness is)
Happiness is
(Happiness is)
Happiness is
(Happiness is)
Different things to different people
That's what happiness is."*

The music may be outdated—I'm pretty sure it always was—but the words still ring true. Happiness depends on things, circumstances, people, experiences—you name it. Different things to different people. This means that when things are bad, we get sad.

Joy is different—at least it can be. Should be. It's not an automatic thing. We are wired for joy by our Creator—but we have to activate it on-demand. And this is a good place to mention that the kind of joy I'm talking about flows from an ultimate and intimate relationship with God.

One day, early during the ministry of Jesus, he and his disciples were on a journey, one that took them through an area known as Samaria. The disciples were a little nervous because, well, Jews like them just didn't go there. It was a thing. But Jesus had a reason for the incursion into a potentially unfriendly neighborhood.

Someone needed him.

He came to a well and soon a local Samaritan woman came by. The disciples had conveniently decided to make a food run, so Jesus was by himself with her. They started a conversation that quickly turned to spiritual things. It was his thing. He told the woman about something called "living water"—contrasting it with water from the nearby well.

"Everyone who drinks this water will be thirsty again, but whoever drinks the water I give him will never thirst. Indeed, the water I give him will become in him a spring of water welling up to eternal life."[3]

Jesus was describing salvation as a well of water *within* us. Whenever Jesus spoke about joy, he described it as an internal thing. Just before his death on the cross, he prayed for his followers, "that they may have the full measure of my joy *within* them."[4]

---

3 John 4:13-14, New International Version.

4 John 17:13, New International Version.

So you could say it like this: Happiness is an *outside* thing. Joy is an *inside* thing. Happiness is about what's happening *to* us. Joy is about what's happening *in* us.

What makes me happy? Family. Good food. Fun stuff. Nice weather. Walk-off home runs. Sinking a long putt. Car trips with Karen. My mother-in-law's coleslaw. Actually, any dish made by my mother-in-law. My cat. British mysteries on *Netflix*. Books. More books. A full moon. A morning star. A word of encouragement. Trumpets. My favorite chair. My second favorite chair. A big snow day—or week. Preaching. Writing.

But there are things that can never make me happy—in fact, they chase happiness far away. Pain. Suffering. Abuse. Storms. Attack. Rejection. Death.

They destroy happiness, but they can't kill joy. Only I can do that by my attitudes and with my choices.

I've experienced joy at funerals. I've known joy in the midst of pain. I've learned to experience joy when life, well, pardon my language, but when life sucks.

Happiness is fine, but you can't depend on it. It's cool, but it comes and goes.

The great challenge of life is to constantly, at every turn, choose joy, especially when we're not happy. Happiness always fades away. It changes as circumstances change. Sometimes the wind blows favorably, and other times it blows contrary. Happiness is as dependent on circumstances as a sailboat is to the wind.

Joy, however, is the real deal. Whether there is wind, no wind—or even a fierce storm.

And here's the awesome thing—we can choose joy every moment of every day.

So just how do we tap into the power of joy in real-time?

Joy is triggered when we *make the choice to rejoice.*

There is a powerful scene at the end of HBO's *John Adams* miniseries in which Adams demonstrates the choice to rejoice. The production was based on David McCullough's Pulitzer Prize-winning biography about one of the founding fathers of our nation. Adams was a very successful lawyer and statesman. He was the second President of the United States. Yet he also knew his share of heartbreak. One of his sons died an alcoholic. His daughter died of cancer.

The HBO scene shows Adams walking through a cornfield with his son. Adams remarks: "Still, still I am not weary of life. Strangely. I have hope. You take away hope and what remains? What pleasures? I have seen a queen of France with eighteen million livres of diamonds on her person, but I declare that all the charms of her face and figure, added to all the glitter of her jewels, did not impress me as much as that little shrub. *[pointing with his walking stick to a small white flower in the field]* Now my mother always said that I never delighted enough in the mundane, but now I find that if I look at even the smallest thing, my imagination begins to roam the Milky Way. Rejoice evermore. Rejoice Evermore! It's a phrase from St. Paul, you fool! REJOICE EVERMORE! I wish that had always been in my heart and on my tongue. I am filled with an irresistible impulse to fall on my knees right here in admiration."

God is never going to force joy on us. He is not going to force-feed it. Joy starts with our choice to reject cynicism and negativism. In that moment, even if it is contrary (*especially* if it's contrary), we make a choice that says, "I am, by faith, rejoicing because God wants me to."

God commands us to rejoice. The Scriptures tell us to, "Rejoice evermore." "In everything, give thanks and rejoice."[5] We have to organize our thoughts around a new pattern. We need to pray something like this, "I don't feel that way right now, God. I'm surely not happy, because look at this circumstance, but you tell me to rejoice in everything. I'm choosing joy. I'm doing it by faith. I'm admitting my weakness."

When we do that—when we surrender to God in the joyless moment—we are properly positioned to experience supernatural joy. The Holy Spirit lives in followers of Jesus,[6] but it takes surrender and faith to experience the "fruit" of that relationship.[7]

Something happened while I was writing this chapter—something that challenged my joy. So, I had to stop and choose joy again— sort of a reboot. I deliberately rejoiced in the face of a less-than-happy circumstance. I had to transform how I felt about what had

---

[5] I Thessalonians 5:16-18, New International Version

[6] Romans 8:9, New International Version

[7] Galatians 5:22, New International Version

happened. I prayed, "Father, I'm not happy with this, but right now I am choosing to rejoice."

He answered that prayer immediately—it was amazing!

Think on These Things

Describe how JOY & HAPPINESS are different.

How does the cultivation of authentic joy strengthen my spiritual life?

What is God's role in joy, and what is my responsibility?

What did Jesus mean when he talked about "living water" with the Samaritan woman?

How do we "activate" the joy of the Lord?

READING:
Philippians 1:1-18
Romans 5:1-5
Psalm 16
Romans 8:32-38

CHAPTER TWO

Jailhouse Joy

The Bible has a lot to say about joy. Several centuries before Christ was born, a great servant-leader named Nehemiah spoke to his countrymen during challenging times and said, "The joy of the Lord is your strength."[8]

This makes sense. After all, our attitudes affect our actions. We tend to be more productive when we are joyful.

Colonel Saito, the iron-willed commandant of a World War II Japanese prison camp in Burma in the epic movie, *Bridge on the River Kwai*, tried to motivate the prisoners of war under his charge to "be happy in your work." That work was the building of a strategic bridge to help the enemy's war effort, so the captured men weren't all that happy. Who could be under such circumstances?

Of course, the story was *fictional.*

---

[8] Nehemiah 8:10, New International Version.

Dietrich Bonhoeffer, meanwhile, was a real-life POW in Germany. He was a German patriot—a man of faith and courage—and was willing to speak and work against Hitler's tyranny and the wickedness of the Nazi regime at the risk of his own safety and life. Yet, even while many of his friends were dying (he would be executed in 1945), and others were suffering for their faith, he reminded anyone who would listen: "Joy abides with God, and it comes down from God and embraces spirit, soul, and body; and where this joy has seized a person, there it spreads, there it carries one away, there it bursts open closed doors."[9]

Joy—even in prison.

Joy—even when God gives you a "time out."

Enter a man named Paul. He spent a lot of time behind bars, or at least in confinement, sometimes with chains. I think it was God's way of slowing him down to give him time to receive and reflect on vital revelation. He was an apostle, preacher, church planter, evangelist, and bold ambassador for Christ in high places. But none of the churches he started are around anymore.

We do, however, still have what he wrote.

I write in a nice office at my home. I have a large church office—filled with books. But I don't write there. Too many interruptions. Okay, to be fair, I'm the interrupter. Whenever people are in the outer office or hallway outside my door, I just have to find out what

---

[9] *Dietrich Bonhoeffer Works*, vol. 16, *Conspiracy and Imprisonment: 1940–1945* (Fortress, 2006), p. 377

they're doing and saying. Working at home protects me from such temptation.

Unless there are grandkids in the house.

I'm sitting at my writing desk right now (in case you're wondering—it's nothing like a raven)[10]. A large computer screen is in front of me. To my left is a bay window area. I can see our entire *cul de sac*. Yep, I keep my eye on things. Nothing gets past me. People come and go. I have all their license numbers. The mailman just ran his vehicle into a garbage can.

Again.

To my right is a wall of books—well, actually, the wall is made of wood and sheetrock, but there are shelves with books by it. These are the works I keep at hand for writing projects—and coloring.

I love my home office. It's one of my happy places, because happiness is about things and places. I'm writing right now—but of course, you knew that. Next to preaching, writing is my favorite work. I'm so glad to have a special place to write.

In 1945, a Soviet Red Army soldier named Alexander Solzhenitsyn was arrested for criticizing the dictator Joseph Stalin in a private letter to a friend. He was sentenced to eight years of hard labor in a Siberian camp. He began to hoard scraps of paper so he could make notes about his experiences. Eight years later, he was released from prison, and nearly a decade after that he turned those scraps

---

[10] "Why is a raven like a writing desk?", The Mad Hatter, "Alice in Wonderland"

and notes into a great novel titled, *One Day in the Life of Ivan Denisovich*. He was later awarded the Nobel Prize for Literature.

Pretty good prison writing.

Gandhi wrote his autobiography in prison. So did Nelson Mandela. And, of course, there is *Orange is the New Black*, but I digress.

Without question, the greatest prison writing in history was done by the Apostle Paul, during two protracted periods of confinement in Rome. During the first such time-out, he wrote a letter to some very special people. They populated a fledgling church in a place called Philippi. Paul's Epistle to the Philippians, or simply, The Book of Philippians, is not a lengthy letter, nor would you call it a treatise—but it is powerful.

It's all about JOY.

I think I would have a hard time writing about joy if I were in jail. I have a hard time even breaking into a smile during a traffic jam. I pull out of gas stations when the lines are too long—even if my car is running on fumes. When I do get to a pump, if it is running too slow, I cut it off at half a tank. It shouldn't take so long to pump gas. They just want you to watch that video commercial or go inside and buy something. I'm way too smart—and impatient—for that. Wait for an hour to get into a restaurant? Seriously? I'm with the late philosopher Yogi Berra: "No one goes to that place anymore, it's too crowded." I was once a young man in a hurry. Now, I'm not so young—but I'm still in a hurry. I have to be the first away from the traffic light when it turns green. I win.

Paul, though, had the capacity to turn his prison into a palace. The jailhouse became a joy-house. And, get this—he wrote to the brethren in Philippi to encourage *them*.

Recently, someone battling a life-threatening illness asked me how *I* was feeling.

Philippi was a strategic city in those days, "a Macedonian hill town overlooking the coastal plain and the bay at Neapolis."[11] It was founded by and named for Philip II of Macedon, the father of Alexander the Great. It became a crucial connection to Proconsular Asia (modern day Turkey) and Europe. It was the site of a battle between Antony, Brutus, and Cassius. Back then, if you wanted to talk trash to an enemy or opponent, you'd say:

"I'll meet you at Philippi."

It was even better than a triple-dog dare.

In the first century, Philippi was a Roman colony—sort of a mini Rome six hundred miles to the east. A majority of the residents of Philippi were Roman citizens. In those days, citizens of Rome paid no taxes. It was a pretty sweet deal.

The Apostle Paul and his ministry team went to Philippi.[12] There were very few Jews in town. The first thing Paul usually did when he hit town was to visit the local synagogue. The pattern had been established—start at the synagogue, and then go from there. However, there was no synagogue in Philippi. You see, in order to

---

11 "Exploring Philippians," by John Phillips, p. 9

12 See: Acts 16:12-40, New International Version

establish a synagogue, it required ten Jewish men. Why? Because the tithes of ten men could support a rabbi.

How's that for a church-planting idea?

There weren't ten Jewish men in the city of Philippi in 50 AD. But there were a few devout Jewish women. Worshippers with no synagogue. What did they do? They did what small groups of Jewish worshippers had been doing since the days of the seventy-year Babylonian exile hundreds of years earlier. They found a place down by the river.

"By the rivers of Babylon, we sat and wept when we remembered Zion. There on the poplars we hung our harps, for there our captors asked us for songs, our tormentors demanded songs of joy; they said, 'Sing us one of the songs of Zion!' How can we sing the songs of the Lord while in a foreign land? If I forget you, Jerusalem, may my right hand forget its skill. May my tongue cling to the roof of my mouth if I do not remember you, if I do not consider Jerusalem my highest joy."[13]

One particular Sabbath morning, a few women, led by a successful entrepreneur, made their way out of Philippi's city gate toward the River Krenides. They found their customary spot and began to pray. Lydia—the businesswoman—led the group. She had moved to Philippi from a place called Thyatira—a city located south of what is now called Istanbul in western Turkey. She was in the clothing business—her specialty was garments dyed purple, a

---

13 Psalm 137:1-6, New International Version

signature brand from her hometown. Lydia was not a Jew by birth, but she was a "God-fearer" and a convert to the religion.

She was also quite wealthy.

Here's how Dr. Luke described what happened:

"On the Sabbath we went outside the city gate to the river, where we expected to find a place of prayer. We sat down and began to speak to the women who had gathered there. One of those listening was a woman from the city of Thyatira named Lydia, a dealer in purple cloth. She was a worshiper of God. The Lord opened her heart to respond to Paul's message. When she and the members of her household were baptized, she invited us to her home. 'If you consider me a believer in the Lord,' she said, 'come and stay at my house.' And she persuaded us."[14]

Soon, others were converted and controversy followed—the kind that seems always to dog those trying to do the right thing. Paul and his assistant were arrested and thrown in jail. But it didn't matter because they had the joy of the Lord as their strength. In fact, even while incarcerated they rejoiced and sang joyful songs. The guard who was charged to watch them was impressed—consciously and subconsciously. In fact, God was using the prisoners to preach to the jailer, and the message got through, even as he slept.

On a side note, as a preacher, I've always been encouraged by the fact that the gospel could convict a *sleeping* man—just saying.

---

[14] Acts 16:13-15, New International Version

God moved powerfully; the jailor and his family were gloriously saved.

A new church was born.

Now, a decade or so later, Paul must have smiled at the irony. A prison in Philippi became a birthing place for a church; now he was in yet another prison writing back to his dear friends.

And he was still filled with joy.

Think on These Things

What does it mean to cultivate joy, even when I don't feel like it?

What has been my greatest personal experience with joy?

What has been the happiest moment of my life?

Have I ever decided to be joyful even while unhappy?

Why do you think God allowed Paul to spend so much time in prison?

READING:
Philippians 1:19-30
Acts 16:12-40

CHAPTER THREE

When the Wheels Fall Off

A few years earlier, while ministering in the city of Corinth, Paul wrote a majestic letter to the Christians in Rome. He told them that he couldn't wait to visit them—to visit Rome. He said he longed to see what God was doing in the lives of His people in the most powerful city in the world. He had heard of their faith and wanted to visit them, but plans never seemed to work out.[15]

Even beyond his heartfelt desire to *minister* in Rome, there can be no doubt that Paul wanted to see the city *itself*. He was a man of God, but also a man of the world—not in the sense of being attracted to the world system, but rather as a strategic thinker with a global vision for the gospel. He was well-traveled and well-read.

Paul was an omni-visionary.

Rome was London, New York, Paris, Mexico City, and Johannesburg rolled into one—and so much more. No place on

---
[15] See: Romans 1:7-13, New International Version

earth like it, back then. Some historians suggest a first-century population of two or three *million* in the city and its surrounding towns.[16] It was imperial, grand, powerful, and crowded. The city had grown dramatically from its ancient form and through the years of the Republic. By Paul's day, it was the center of a vast and powerful empire.

Imperial Rome came about largely due to the efforts of Gaius Octavius—we know him as Caesar Augustus. His reign ushered in an era known as *Pax Romana* ("the Roman peace"), creating the politically stable environment for Christ's life and ministry, as well as the beginnings of His church. When Augustus died in 14 AD, he reputedly said: "I found Rome brick, and I leave it marble."[17]

Rome was the capital of planet earth.

A series of "Caesars" followed Augustus. By the time Paul arrived in Rome, a man named Nero was in charge—*Nero Claudius Caesar Augustus Germanicus.* He would mess things up so badly, the hereditary dynasty ("Julio-Claudian") ended when he was overthrown. But that usurpation was too little and too late to save Paul from losing his head—literally.

Back in 1979, the crooner Frank Sinatra came out of yet-another retirement to score a big hit song—"New York, New York." A line of the lyrics said, *"If I can make it there, I'll make it anywhere."* To succeed in the Big Apple—in business, entertainment, and even in ministry—is tough. I know, I've tried it. But if you can somehow

---

16 *Archaeology and the New Testament.* Grand Rapids, by Merrill Unger, p. 319

17 http://www.archaeology.org/news/3058-150304-rome-brick-marble

"make it" there, well, you've got the stuff to succeed anywhere. It's like a litmus test for difficulty—the ultimate "tough room."

Rome was that kind of place. But when Paul finally made it there, no songs were sung about it. Nobody said, *"Start spreading the news..."*. Paul didn't hit town—the town hit him.

Let me explain—"no, there is too much. Let me sum up."[18]

Paul ended his third missionary journey with a visit to Jerusalem, even though there were clear indications that The Holy City had become dangerous a place for him. Some even tried to talk him out of the trip, but he insisted, *"I am ready not only to be bound, but also to die in Jerusalem for the name of the Lord Jesus."*[19]

Among those with Paul was a man named Trophimus. He was from Ephesus. His name would be associated with a great falsehood and miscarriage of justice because some of the Jewish worshippers from Ephesus recognized Trophimus. Later, when Paul was in the Temple, the Ephesian men assumed Paul had brought Trophimus *into* the Temple, which would have been a big violation of Jewish law and custom. In fact, Paul never brought his Greek friend to the Temple, but the accusation was enough. The Bible says, *"The whole city was aroused, and the people came running from all directions."*[20]

You gotta love angry protesters with less-than-factual information.

---

18 Inigo Montoya in "The Princess Bride," 1987

19 Acts 21:13, New International Version

20 Acts 21:30, New International Version

Things quickly spiraled out of control. Many people wanted Paul killed—on the spot—but Roman soldiers intervened, beginning a lengthy process that ultimately took Paul to Rome. The charges brought by his countrymen were false and convoluted and made no sense to Roman authorities.

But there were forty men in Jerusalem who were conspiring to murder Paul. When the Romans caught wind of the plot, they arranged for him to be transported from the city under heavy guard in the middle of the night. Along the way, Paul shared his testimony, invoked his Roman citizenship—always an attention-grabbing game-changer—and had audiences with a number of Roman officials of increasing power and importance.

When he finally set out for Rome, it was on a ship as one of more than 250 hardened criminals. The trip was long, tedious, at times turbulent, and yet, fruitful. He survived storms (including a nor'easter), a deadly snakebite, the wrath of mutinous mariners, a shipwreck—all with supernatural power. He witnessed. He prayed. He taught. He healed.

"And so, we came to Rome."[21]

This should be remembered as Paul's *fourth* missionary journey. Paul learned about what he was getting into—the kind of bi-polar experience he would have—within days of his conversion. The first man to embrace him after his Damascus road encounter was a fellow named Ananias. Through him, Paul heard all about his future. *"The Lord said to Ananias, 'Go! This man is my chosen instrument to carry my name before the Gentiles <u>and their kings</u>*

---

21 Acts 28:14, New International Version

and before the people of Israel. I will show him how much he must suffer for my name.'[22] The treacherous travel to Rome involved all aspects of Paul's God-given purpose—even the suffering.

Especially the suffering.

It would be easy to put Paul on a pedestal and see him in completely heroic terms—a man of unceasing courage and unwavering inner-calm. But that would be a mistake. As James described the prophet Elijah as a man with "passions" like us,[23] so Paul was very human. There is ample Biblical evidence that he battled insecurity, hyper-sensitivity—even depression.[24]

Joy was not his default position—nor is it ours. To rejoice always involves a deliberate choice.

I find it interesting that when Paul arrived in Rome and was met by a few brothers in Christ, the Scriptures record: *"At the sight of these men Paul thanked God and was encouraged."*[25] He was down, and they lifted his spirits.

One more thing about Paul's first trip to Rome. This was the first of two imprisonments in the city. It would last for two years. A few years later, he'd be back. The two experiences were quite different. His next "visit" would be much more severe. He'd be on death row. Nero would want his head.

---

[22] Acts 9:15-16, New International Version

[23] James 5:17, King James Version

[24] The author believes these "weaknesses" were what he meant by his comments about "a thorn in the flesh." See: II Corinthians chapters 11 & 12 and note the connection.

[25] Acts 28:15, New International Version

This first experience, however, was not as extreme. He was, in effect, under *house arrest*. Confined, but not brutalized. *"When he got to Rome, Paul was allowed to live by himself, with a soldier to guard him."*[26]

It wasn't the gulag, but it was grueling. It wasn't hard-labor, but it was harrowing. It wasn't a house of horrors, but it was a hurtful place. It wasn't dangerous, but it was discouraging. It wasn't frightening, but it was frustrating.

"For two whole years Paul stayed there in his own rented house and welcomed all who came to see him. He proclaimed the kingdom of God and taught about the Lord Jesus Christ—with all boldness and without hindrance!"[27]

He also wrote four books of the New Testament during that "down time": Ephesians, Philemon, Colossians—and a very personal letter to the Philippians.

---

[26] Acts 28:16, New International Version

[27] Acts 28:30-31, New International Version

Think on These Things

Why did Paul want to go to Rome?

How do I handle it when God makes other plans?

Did Paul have a death-wish?

How often was Paul treated unfairly?

How did Paul's earliest discipleship training prepare him for suffering?

READING:
Romans 1:7-13
Acts 21:13-30
Acts 9
Acts 28:15-31

CHAPTER FOUR

Joy & Remembrance

The human mind is amazing. There are people who study just how amazing our brains are—they're called computational neuroscientists. These real-life brainiacs estimate the average human brain has a storage capacity of somewhere between ten and one hundred *terabytes*. One terabyte is equal to one *million* megabytes.[28]

Talk about being "wonderfully made."[29]

If we're not very interested in a topic, most adults have an attention span of twenty minutes. So, chances are, you're not reading this. Left-handed people have better memories. Short-term memories

---

28

http://www.slate.com/articles/health_and_science/explainer/2012/04/north_korea_s_2_mb_of_knowledge_taunt_how_many_meg abytes_does_the_human_brain_hold_.html

29 Psalm 139:14, New International Version

can hold seven pieces of information at the same time—but only for twenty seconds. We average about 70,000 thoughts every day.[30]

If you're like me, only three or four of them are any good.

We analyze with our brains. We imagine with our brains. We calculate with our brains. And we remember with our brains. Memories can haunt us or help us. Dwelling on painful things from the past leads to depression and despair. On the other hand, remembering pleasant experiences can lift our spirits.

As the Apostle Paul began his letter to his friends in Philippi, he used a skill I call *sanctified recall*. Using memory as an aid to spiritual health and, yes, to fuel joy. He wrote:

"Paul and Timothy, servants of Christ Jesus, To all God's holy people in Christ Jesus at Philippi, together with the overseers and deacons: Grace and peace to you from God our Father and the Lord Jesus Christ. I thank my God every time I remember you. In all my prayers for all of you, I always pray with joy because of your partnership in the gospel from the first day until now, being confident of this, that he who began a good work in you will carry it on to completion until the day of Christ Jesus. It is right for me to feel this way about all of you, since I have you in my heart and, whether I am in chains or defending and confirming the gospel, all of you share in God's grace with me. God can testify how I long for all of you with the affection of Christ Jesus. And this is my prayer: that your love may abound more and more in knowledge and depth of insight, so that you may be able to discern what is best and may be pure and blameless for the day of Christ, filled with the fruit

---

[30] https://southtree.com/memories-matter/statistics-about-human-memory

of righteousness that comes through Jesus Christ—to the glory and praise of God."[31]

Did you notice the connection Paul made between remembrance and gratitude?

He told them that every time an image of one of them—or all of them—popped up on the screen of his imagination, he was driven to heart-felt gratitude. He was joyful.

I have no doubt that he was remembering specific people and particular experiences. Even though he wasn't in Philippi for very long, his visit there was intense and fruitful.

You may need a little more background.

Paul was directly or indirectly involved in the establishment of many churches, but the one at Philippi was special. There was a connection between them and him that was out of proportion to the usual markers of a relationship. Theirs seemed to be an intimate relationship that remained fervent even years later. No doubt, Paul was a hero to them. And they were near and dear to his heart.

All of this was no doubt refreshed in Paul's memory because of the visit of someone he had likely never met before. His name was Epaphroditus. His name will come up later in this story, but for now, just know that he had been sent by the church at Philippi to Rome for the express purpose of visiting and encouraging Paul. He also came to Rome bearing gifts.

---

[31] Philippians 1:1-10, New International Version

The Apostle's imprisonment at this point was more of a house arrest. This is not to say that it was easy—clearly, it wasn't. But he was allowed to have visitors and communicating with those on the outside wasn't all that difficult.

Epaphroditus shared the latest news from Philippi—how things were going. This brought joy to Paul's heart. *"I thank my God every time I remember you."*

Karen and I met at college in 1975. When we began dating, we agreed to meet for breakfast every morning in the school cafeteria—6:00 a.m. For about two weeks we met daily. We ate *Cocoa Krispies*. Until one day when I overslept and she was there by herself and not happy about it. The next day, I made sure to show up and you guessed it, she wasn't there. We stopped meeting for breakfast at that hour, but we retained our love for *Cocoa Krispies*.

It was our thing.

I told that story 30 years ago when I was pastoring in New York. A dear lady named Harriet heard me, and thereafter bring Karen coupons for *Cocoa Krispies* almost every Sunday. We never paid full price for our sugary love cereal. Harriet was a blessing. She is with the Lord now. Every time I think of Harriet, I thank God.

It's like that.

Now there are some people from my past who, when I think about them, my first instinct is not always to thank God. Sanctified recall is selective, or better—*discerning*. We have to learn how to forget some things.

Karen and I were watching a television show recently where this doctor had a way of erasing certain memories—especially inconvenient ones. As I watched, I wondered if he was in my health plan network, because there are some memories, painful ones, I'd just as soon, well, *forget.* That's not really possible under normal mental health circumstances. But there are ways to keep the painful stuff in check.

One way to practice sanctified recall is when negative memories rear their ugly heads, replace them with pleasant memories. So, when a face pops up on the screen of my mind—the face of someone who has hurt me in the past—I shift mental gears. I deliberately, in that same moment, create a mental image of someone like Harriet—and I imagine her getting bigger and bigger on my mental screen, while the painful image gets smaller and smaller and moves down and off—like a computer screen with a trash file. Poof.

And I thank the Lord for Harriet.

Have you ever talked to somebody who grew up during the Great Depression—I mean, back in the 1930s when nobody had anything?

The coolest people in life to talk to are older people—especially if they have a cheerful, positive attitude. They'll tell you, "Oh man, it was great back then. Families were close. We used the same bathwater, shared underwear. I mean, we didn't have much, but we were close." They'll talk about it almost in glowing terms, and meanwhile I'm thinking, "Seriously? That was a *good* time?"

I think they may be forgetting a few things. Selectively. Conveniently. Maybe that's a good thing. Maybe that's a bad thing. But that's the nature of memory. We can weed out all of those bad experiences and select the good ones. This, however, must be done on purpose.

I have no doubt that during moments of frustration and discouragement, the Apostle Paul turned his Roman house into a time machine, going back to places like Philippi and remembering some precious people.

Earlier, I mentioned my mother's hi-fi and the records she liked to play. She had an album recorded by a singer named Tennessee Ernie Ford. He had a deep baritone voice—smooth as silk. I vividly remember hearing him sing a wonderful old hymn:

"Precious memories, unseen angels,
Sent from somewhere to my soul.
How they linger, ever near me,
And the sacred past unfolds.
Precious memories how they linger,
How they ever flood my soul.
In the stillness, of the midnight.
Precious sacred scenes unfold."[32]

The music is from another era. Sure, it's a bit sentimental—even sappy. But sometimes it's exactly what we need—precious memories.

---

[32] Written by Johnnie R. Wright • Copyright © Universal Music Publishing Group

Think on These Things

What is sanctified recall?

Think about people who inspire gratitude & thankfulness in your heart.

How many Bible verses do I know by heart—either word-for-word or paraphrased? (Write them down.)

If I can remember song lyrics, sports stats, and funny movie dialogue, why is it so hard for me to memorize or remember scripture?

Am I willing to start letting the Word become flesh in my life? Could I memorize just one life-changing verse of scripture per week for the next year? (Correct answer: YES)

READING:
Philippians 1:19-30
John 1:1-14
Colossians 3:15-17
Romans 12:1-2
II Corinthians 3:16—4:18
Hebrews 4:12
Hebrews 5:11-14

CHAPTER FIVE

Cheerful in Chains

Admit it—joy is seldom your first response when circumstances surround and squeeze you. Joy must be triggered and cultivated—it must be summoned, invited into our contrary moments.

Like when the Lord puts you in a prolonged "time out."

"It is right for me to feel this way about all of you, since I have you in my heart and, whether I am in chains or defending and confirming the gospel, all of you share in God's grace with me. God can testify how I long for all of you with the affection of Christ Jesus.

And this is my prayer: that your love may abound more and more in knowledge and depth of insight, so that you may be able to discern what is best and may be pure and blameless for the day of Christ, filled with the fruit of righteousness that comes through Jesus Christ—to the glory and praise of God.

Now I want you to know, brothers and sisters, that what has happened to me has actually served to advance the gospel. As a result, it has become clear throughout the whole palace guard and to everyone else that I am in chains for Christ. And because of my chains, most of the brothers and sisters have become confident in the Lord and dare all the more to proclaim the gospel without fear."[33]

How does Paul experience joy when his basic freedom has been unjustly taken from him and he is in chains?

He learns how to make his "prison" a "prism" through which to view his life and purpose. This man who was once accused of turning the world upside down,[34] has learned how to turn his circumstances upside down. He stands them on their head. He turns negatives into positives. He mocks the presence of chains with persistent cheer. The power that transformed him from a malicious and murderous persecutor of the followers of Jesus is now used to change reality. His confinement becomes a badge of honor—a platform for the proclamation of the gospel.

He inspires other believers.

He even influences the palace guard.

Hard to stop someone who is just crazy enough to think every knock is a boost.

The palace guard, known as the Praetorian Guard or the Roman Imperial Guard. This elite force was first formed by Augustus,

---

[33] Philippians 1:7-14, New International Version

[34] Acts 17:6, King James Version

before the birth of Christ. Originally made up of about 10,000 of the finest men in the Roman military, by Paul's time the number was closer to 20,000, dispersed throughout the empire.

Becoming a member of the palace guard was a big deal. It meant you were the best of the best. You served for sixteen years, then when you retired, you received a nice financial reward as well as Roman citizenship—which meant you didn't have to pay taxes.[35]

A few members of this select group of world-class warriors guarded Paul day after day, much of the time being chained to him. The Apostle, instead of bemoaning his plight, chose to use it to bear witness of the power of the gospel.

If you're the kind of person who is always waiting for golden opportunities to do what you know God wants you to do, God will never give you all green lights and sunshine. In fact, the best way to make sure you have that opportunity is to bloom where you're planted now, and to choose joy in your circumstance. If you whine, "Oh, if I only had a better job, if I only had a better house, if the economy." That means you are looking for happiness in what's happening.

Paul gave us an example: Make the choice to rejoice even if you're in prison. Even in spite of contrary circumstances, count it all joy. Add it up and say, "This is all going to equal joy."

God has you right where you are for a reason. It doesn't mean you can't try to improve yourself, because God gives us ideas and ambitions. I get that. But when God closes the door and it's clear

---

[35] "The Letters to the Philippians, Colossians, and Thessalonians," by William Barclay, p. 25

he doesn't want us to do anything else right now, then we must stick it out, choose joy—and bloom.

No matter what.

There are many contrary circumstances that come our way, things that seem to confine us, but we must learn this truth: *Never let what confines you define you.* Make a choice even if you don't feel like it. Choose joy by faith, and God will flood that little speck of joy with his great power and swell it up to where it fills your heart.

Then it can overflow to others.

Think on These Things

How have I let what has confined me, define me?

Why and how does the Lord use "time-outs" to grow us?

Why should my joy be overflowing?

READING:
Philippians 1:7-14
Galatians 1:6-10, 3:1-5, 5:1-26
Colossians 2:11-23
Psalm 23

CHAPTER SIX

Joy, Jerks, and Jealousy

Often the greatest challenges to joyful living come from, well, let's just say it: PEOPLE.

"**Elaine:** Ugh, I hate people. **Jerry:** Yeah, they're the worst.[36]"

As we look back on Paul's experience, we see a hero of the faith. He's a remarkable man—a real role model. But not all of his contemporaries saw him that way. And I'm not just talking about the unredeemed people who persecuted him because they rejected the idea of Jesus as Christ the Lord. There were many Christians who were critical of Paul. I think this bothered him greatly, and perpetually challenged his sense of joy, but he always worked through it.

"It is true that some preach Christ out of envy and rivalry, but others out of goodwill. The latter do so out of love, knowing that I

---

[36] "Seinfeld," season 6, episode 23
Broadcast date: May 11, 1995

am put here for the defense of the gospel. The former preach Christ out of selfish ambition, not sincerely, supposing that they can stir up trouble for me while I am in chains. But what does it matter? The important thing is that in every way, whether from false motives or true, Christ is preached. And because of this I rejoice."[37]

Let me explain to you what I think was happening. As Paul endured his confinement, there were many preachers free to do the Lord's work. And it was likely that some of those "clergymen" fell into a very human trap, one all preachers deal with at times—the development of a critical spirit. I'd love to tell you that those of us in vocational ministry never drift into pettiness or battles over issues of personality or preference. But I can't. I know there have been times when I have been caught up in criticisms about other men of God, other churches, movements, even denominations.

Men of God should be bigger than that—but sometimes we are sadly small.

I suppose a measure of this can be explained by sincere differences of opinion over issues that are perceived as crucial. I mean, when Martin Luther was criticizing the Pope and certain un-Biblical practices, that was pretty important. It changed history. But, if we're honest, much of our criticism of other brethren who don't see or do things just the way we prefer doesn't rise to the level of The Great Reformation.

I grew up a strict Independent Fundamental Baptist (IFB). I always temper my comments with a caveat—I am grateful for many parts of that upbringing, namely an emphasis on Biblical doctrine,

---

[37] Philippians 1:15-19, New International Version

scripture memorization, and personal evangelism. But those positive things often came with negative baggage. Usually, it had to do with culture and a seemingly-endless list of rules and regulations—the kind of list that would make any first-century Pharisee salivate. But there was another "unseemly" aspect to that approach to Christian living—the spirit of criticism.

Anyone not IFB was fair-game.

Sometimes the criticism (in the name of "separatism") became the main thing. I'd go to youth rallies and church meetings and hear denunciations of godless communists, liberal atheists, and modernists. And a favorite punching bag whenever some preachers couldn't think of someone to criticize was—wait for it—Billy Graham.

Yep, *that* Billy Graham.

You see, even though Billy was a Baptist, he wasn't "Baptist" enough. Even though he preached the gospel, he was accused of "watering it down." Even though thousands of people were converted when he preached, most of them weren't "really" saved. So the talking points went.

Looking back on it now, it seems almost surreal. Billy Graham's ministry shook the world for Christ. His life had been blameless. How does it happen that someone as great-for-God as Billy Graham could be criticized as, well, almost an enemy of the cross?

Paul's reference to his critics reminds us that such things are nothing new. What happened to Paul happened to Billy Graham and continues to happen to high profile servants of God in our day.

The next time you hear a preacher criticized by another preacher ask yourself this: Is the Christian leader being criticized in some way more prominent, successful (by numerical standards), or gifted than the one doing the criticizing?

Often, it's as basic as that.

You may resist what I'm saying, "Surely you can't believe that preachers will criticize others for such petty reasons?" Sadly, that's exactly what I'm saying. I know it's true, because I've been guilty of this very thing.

When I was ordained (1977) and began to pastor, I found it easy to find ways to diminish the fruit of other ministries. It was easy to try to build myself up by tearing someone else down. What changed me? Simple—eventually I was the one being criticized. It gave me a whole new perspective. I remember spending some time in prayer, confessing my arrogance and spirit of criticism. Yes, there are times when I, as a pastor, need to speak out about an issue or help people become discerning, but when I do so I must always guard my heart.

Petty is never pretty.

I've been around preachers all my life. I love them. When I was growing up, my heroes were great preachers, past and present—and of course, Al Kaline of the Detroit Tigers. But I know clergymen can be competitive—even jealous at times.

In the Summer of 1941, a twenty-seven-year-old preacher moved his family from California to the heart of the American Midwest to assume his duties as the new pastor of a young and vibrant church.

The church was only five-years-old, but it had experienced significant growth under the leadership of its popular founding pastor. He was leaving to pursue his passion to become a full-time evangelist. The new pastor was the founder's handpicked successor, a choice ratified by a near-unanimous vote of the congregation.

A few months later, the founding minister returned for a visit and the new pastor invited him to the pulpit to say a few words of greeting. As the founding pastor approached the pulpit, the audience stood and gave him a prolonged ovation. The new pastor instantly felt his heart sink. He had never received such a reception. He found himself filled with jealousy, and it bothered him—not just the ovation itself, but his visceral response. He knew envy was one of the perils of the ministry and he had to conquer it. He prayed about it, and the Lord impressed him with a solution. He was scheduled soon to be gone for four Sundays in a row, so he decided to face his problem head on.

He invited his predecessor to fill the pulpit all four of those upcoming Sundays.

Decades later, the preacher would tell his Pastoral Theology students—including me—that the moment he extended the invitation to his predecessor, he was released from bondage to the spirit of envy. And every time he told the story, he would pause and smile, adding that on his first Sunday back after that four-week absence, the congregation gave *him* a standing ovation.[38]

---

[38] "Cry Aloud, Spare Not: The Story of W.E. Dowell," by Stephen E. Dowell, Pilgrimage Road Press, p. 90

By the way, criticism is not just a preacher problem; it's a people problem. So, check your heart the next time you're tempted to tear someone else down in order to build yourself up.

There's no joy in that.

Think on These Things

Have I ever heard preaching that was excessively critical of other ministries?

Have I ever had a critical spirit?

When was the last time I really examined my spiritual condition and evaluated the condition of my relationship with the Lord?

When was the last time I was petty?

READING:
Philippians 1:15-19
Hebrews 5:11-14
II Peter 1:3-11
Romans 12:1-2
Any good biography of Billy Graham

CHAPTER SEVEN

Wait for It

As we look back on our lives, we may notice the moments we were happiest tended to involve some*thing* or some*one* else. Something favorable. Something fun. Something unexpected. Something good. Something captivating. Life includes such things. They happen and make us happy. But these moments come and go—they never last.

Joy is different. Joy can be constant. But it has to be understood, chosen, and cultivated in real time.

Here's the key: Joy is most needed when we least *feel* like it.

During the times in our lives when everything turns to crap,[39] when storms rage around and in us, when even the simplest tasks become monumentally hard because discouragement and

---

39 Pardon this, but it's the right word. — DRS

depression have made their home in our hearts, this is when we can experience the most pervasive and profound joy.

"Rejoice evermore."[40]

When you see the word *rejoice* in scripture, it simply means: Choose joy. To rejoice involves a choice. It's a command. It doesn't say, "Rejoice if you feel like it." In fact, true joy needs to be part of our lives when we *least* feel like it. That's one of the marks of spiritual growth, as we move toward spiritual maturity.

Years ago, a psychologist by the name of M. Scott Peck wrote one of the most popular books of the twentieth century, spending more than 700 weeks on the *New York Times* bestseller list. It was a self-help book called *The Road Less Traveled*.[41] Peck described the capacity to defer gratification as the mark of emotional maturity. This is why we try to teach our children (or at least we should) that they can't have everything they want right now.

We're fighting a tough battle in this age of "instant gratification."

As a father and grandfather, I've made significant financial investments in what used to be a vast swampland in the middle of Florida. What was worthless real estate 50 years ago was transformed by a visionary into a giant magnet for people and their hard-earned cash—*Disney World*.

Over the years, I've become increasingly convinced, through my study of scripture and economic trends that the dystopian prophecies in the Book of Revelation about needing a "mark" on

---

[40] I Thessalonians 5:16, King James Version

[41] "The Road Less Traveled: A New Psychology of Love, Traditional Values and Spiritual Growth," M. Scott Peck, 1978

the right hand or forehead to buy or sell refers to an image of mouse ears. I took my whole family down there a while back—including seven grandchildren. *Disney* now has a system where you don't need cash. They give you a magic wristband that connects to Grandpa's credit card. With it you can do anything. It opens the door to your room. You use it to buy anything. It monitors your heartbeat, blood pressure, muscle mass, ancestry—and your net worth.[42]

I'm pretty proud of myself. I fooled them. I put it on my *left* wrist.[43]

By the way, don't tell Vladimir Putin this, but if he really wants to mess with America, he should hack into those sinister wristbands.

What makes all things *Disney* so successful?

Instant gratification.

It's the "happiest place on earth" because everyone can have it all NOW.

Instant gratification is not just a thing in Florida. It's the spirit that governs our present age—the zeitgeist. This is because the world has always been about *lust*.

"Do not love the world or the things in the world. If anyone loves the world, the love of the Father is not in him. For all that is in the world—the lust of the flesh, the lust of the eyes, and the pride of life—is not of the Father but is of the world. And the world is

---

42 Hyperboly. I think.

43 Revelation 13:16-18, New International Version

passing away, and the lust of it; but he who does the will of God abides forever.[44]

Many years ago, I visited my father when he was finishing up a pastorate in Pennsylvania. It was moving day, so I drove over from Long Island[45] to help. When I arrived, I saw a dozen or so men loading the truck. I was relieved. Didn't really want to do any heavy lifting.

My father's ministry always seemed to include a component where he worked with some of the toughest cases—people who had fallen off the grid. I suppose it was because his childhood had been rough. His father had been in prison for twenty years. He had an abusive step-dad. Grew up in the Great Depression. Rough stuff. When he came to Christ in his early twenties, Dad had a soft spot for people who had been dealt a losing hand by life. He took in strays.

When he began preaching, even before his first pastorate, he would go to rescue missions, where broken men lived. Occasionally, he would insist I go with him. Usually as a punishment. The places were horrible. The smell. The sounds. And Dad loved to stay for lunch with the men. He ate whatever they ate.

I didn't.

The men packing his truck that day were the latest example of Dad's outreach to outcasts. They were from a halfway house in the area. Dad had ministered to them, and they were saying thank you

---

44 I John 2:15-17, New King James Version

45 I pastored a church in Westbury, NY from 1986-mid-1998

by helping him. They had substance abuse issues and were going through a program to get clean.

After watching them work for a few minutes, I started feeling guilty about not helping at all. So I said, "Hey, let me go over to the *Burger King* and get you some *Whoppers*." They said, "No, no, Mr. Stokes. No, thank you. We're not allowed to have *Whoppers*."

Not allowed to have *Whoppers*? Maybe, I thought, it was some kind of anti-*Burger King* thing, with its monarchial and imperial imagery. Then I said, "Okay, I'll get *Big Macs*, how's that?"

"No sir, but thank you. Can't have *McDonald's* either."

I was curious. Were they Bolsheviks? Also, I really wanted a hamburger. I then asked, "Are you in some kind of vegetarian program?"

"Oh no, sir. We love meat. We just grow our own in the program. We grow our own vegetables, too. And we have to cook our own food. It's all about breaking our addiction."

"So, this is a twelve-step program for fast food addicts?" I said it hesitantly, in case the man was a recruiter and this was really some kind of intervention for me orchestrated by my wife—or my mother.

He laughed. "No sir. It's a program to help us get over our addiction to *instant gratification*."

How many problems in our lives are compounded by the fact that we have so much at our fingertips?

Think about Noah in the Bible. Long after he built the Ark and survived the great flood, maybe years later, he got depressed and thought, "I feel like getting drunk." What did he do?

"Noah, a man of the soil, proceeded to plant a vineyard."[46]

So "instant" is a relative term.

It takes several years for vines to produce grapes for wine. Sin has always been attractive to human nature, but there was a time when it took longer to get there. A gambling addict 150 years ago had to ride hours, maybe days, to find a card game or roulette table. Now we have the Internet.

It's hard to keep temptation at arm's length when it's right at our fingertips.

In the Christian life, we have to learn how to avoid sacrificing the permanent on the altar of the immediate—and we have to learn how to choose joy, even when we don't feel like it.

How?

Hope.

"For I know that this will turn out for my deliverance through your prayer and the supply of the Spirit of Jesus Christ, according to my earnest expectation and hope that in nothing I shall be ashamed,

---

[46] Genesis 9:20, New International Version

but with all boldness, as always, so now also Christ will be magnified in my body, whether by life or by death."[47]

The Apostle Paul could be joyful because he was filled with hope. He knew the temporary circumstance would not be his permanent situation. Years earlier, he had written this to the believers in Rome—the city where he was now confined:

"For I consider that our present sufferings are not worth comparing with the glory that will be revealed in us."[48]

Paul knew there was a life-lesson even more vital than learning to defer gratification.

He was empowered by deferred *glorification*.

---

[47] Philippians 1:19-20, King James Version

[48] Romans 8:18, New International Version

Think on These Things

How does the pervasive push for "instant gratification" work against true joy?

What is "deferred glorification"?

What is lust?

What drives the world system?

How does "hope" help us?

READING:
Philippians 1:19-20
Romans 8:18-31
I John 2:15

CHAPTER EIGHT

Now & Not Yet

As I mentioned earlier, History tells us Paul went to prison in Rome *twice*—separated by a time of fruitful freedom. He wrote the Book of Philippians during his first Roman incarceration when he was under house arrest. It was captivity, to be sure, but he had a few privileges. As I mentioned earlier, people could come and go. People could minister to him. He could communicate, at least somewhat, with the outside world.

The second time he went to Rome it was very different. He wrote about it in his second letter to Timothy. Paul knew his plight was serious—he knew he was going to die. He waxed philosophical:

"For I am already being poured out like a drink offering, and the time for my departure is near. I have fought the good fight, I have finished the race, I have kept the faith. Now there is in store for me the crown of righteousness, which the Lord, the righteous Judge,

will award to me on that day—and not only to me, but also to all who have longed for his appearing."[49]

His language and tone in his epistle to the Philippians, however, was more upbeat:

"For I know that this will turn out for my deliverance through your prayer and the supply of the Spirit of Jesus Christ, according to my earnest expectation and hope that in nothing I shall be ashamed, but with all boldness, as always, so now also Christ will be magnified in my body, whether by life or by death."[50]

Paul had hope in both cases, though they were so different. God had impressed on Paul that there was still work to be done. He would be set free for a while. But by the time he returned to Rome in chains, he knew that his days on this earth were numbered.

Here's the cool thing, though—Paul was empowered in both circumstances by the same thing—ultimate hope.

Years earlier, he had written to the Roman Christians about this:

"Therefore, since we have been justified through faith, we have peace with God through our Lord Jesus Christ, through whom we have gained access by faith into this grace in which we now stand. And we boast in the hope of the glory of God. Not only so, but we also glory in our sufferings, because we know that suffering produces perseverance; perseverance, character; and character, hope. And hope does not put us to shame, because God's love has

---

[49] II Timothy 4:6-8, New International Version

[50] Philippians 1:19-20, New International Version

been poured out into our hearts through the Holy Spirit, who has been given to us."[51]

And...

"For in this hope we were saved. But hope that is seen is no hope at all. Who hopes for what they already have? But if we hope for what we do not yet have, we wait for it patiently."[52]

Again, deferred glorification.

During both of his imprisonments in Rome, the man in charge of everything was Nero Claudius Caesar Augustus Germanicus. Nero for short. He was a deeply twisted man. He became the most powerful man in the world when he was still a teenager. He had his first wife killed so he could marry his mistress. Then a few weeks later, after his new wife displeased him, he kicked her so hard she died. He was the last of all the Caesars blood-related to Julius Caesar.

Talk about bad blood.

His mother was Agrippina. She was the great-great-granddaughter of Caesar Augustus and the sister of Emperor Caligula, another depraved dude. Agrippina was married to Emperor Claudius. To make room for her son to rule Rome she had to get rid of her husband. Tradition says she fed him poisonous mushrooms. So, Nero became the Emperor of Rome, with mommy behind the throne, pulling the strings.

---

51 Romans 5:1-5, New International Version

52 Romans 8:24-25, New International Version

After a few years, Nero grew weary of mommy dearest. He wanted to be his own man, so he decided to kill Agrippina. He tried to poison her three times. Now, he wasn't the brightest guy, because she'd already demonstrated a proficiency with poison. When he said, "Mom, I made you some mushrooms, my special recipe," she didn't bite.

He then rigged her bed chamber so the whole ceiling would fall in and crush her as she slept. That didn't work. He sent her out to sea and told the mariners to put her in a leaky boat so she could drown. Another epic fail. Finally, he told some of his loyal guards, "Let's just do it the old-fashioned way. Stab her."

That worked.

Paul was in Rome, under arrest, and waiting to see this evil emperor. God had already told him about it during a storm at sea:

"Do not be afraid, Paul. You must stand trial before Caesar."[53]

We're not sure when the face-to-face meeting between the emperor and the evangelist took place. My sense is that Paul's Nero "moment" came during his *second* imprisonment, just before his martyrdom. He referred to his "first defense" just before he died,[54] which would indicate that, by that time, he'd been tried twice. His first trial likely didn't get too far in Rome. The issues didn't really have much to do with the empire, being a largely local Jewish matter. Paul dodged a bullet that time, or as he said it:

---

53 Acts 27:24, New International Version

54 II Timothy 4:16, New International Version

"And I was delivered from the mouth of the lion."[55]

That was probably "code" for being delivered from the wrath of Nero.

By the time he was arrested and brought to Rome the second time, many things had changed. The great fire of Rome had occurred in the interval. That fire, of course, led to mass persecution of Christians. So Paul became an enemy of the state. Also, Seneca, Nero's great mentor and the only person who could have any success keeping his boss's dark side in check, had been forced to commit suicide by Nero. It's possible that Seneca played a role in Paul's release after his first trial.

But with Seneca gone, and Rome in ruins, you can almost hear the voices in the demented despot's head shouting, "Now, let Nero be Nero!" Madness became public policy. Later, probably in AD 68, Paul had his audience with Nero, and it did not go well. He was sentenced to death and eventually beheaded. A few weeks after that, there was a massive revolt against Nero's regime. A short time later, Nero stabbed himself to death. He was 31 years-old.

All that came long after Paul's first arrest and imprisonment. The record shows that he handled both imprisonments the same way.

With abounding joy.

---

[55] II Timothy 4:17, New International Version

Think on These Things

What were the differences between Pauls' first and second Roman imprisonments?

How do we balance hope and patience?

How do we magnify Christ in our lives?

What is the difference between human hope and ultimate hope?

READING:
Philippians 1:19-20
II Timothy 4:1-17
Romans 5:1-8

CHAPTER NINE

Jesus & Joy

The secret of Paul's seemingly endless capacity for joy is actually no secret at all. Jesus was the source. Had been ever since that unforgettable day on that hot and dusty road to Damascus—the day that changed everything for him. His direction. His desires. His destiny. He had a relationship that caused him to rejoice always.

Jesus never stopped being real to him.

He said it this way to the saints at Philippi:

"I eagerly expect and hope that I will in no way be ashamed, but will have sufficient courage so that now as always Christ will be exalted in my body, whether by life or by death. For to me, to live is Christ and to die is gain. If I am to go on living in the body, this will mean fruitful labor for me. Yet what shall I choose? I do not know! I am torn between the two: I desire to depart and be with Christ, which is better by far; but it is more necessary for you that I remain in the body. Convinced of this, I know that I will remain, and I will continue with all of you for your progress and joy in the

faith, so that through my being with you again your boasting in Christ Jesus will abound on account of me.[56]

Paul found joy in the exaltation of Christ.

What does it mean to exalt Christ? It means to make Christ great. To live in such a way that it reflects positively on him. Do you remember what John the Baptist said when he was in prison? *"He must increase; I must decrease."*[57] That's how we are to exalt Christ: to make Christ great before the world.

Paul is choosing joy by embracing the *now* and *not yet* dynamics of his life. A few years later, he would say, "It's over. Fought a good fight, finished my course, kept the faith." Now he's saying, "I long for heaven, but there's still a job to do. There are still things to accomplish." That's healthy.

When I was in Bible college, a big theory made the rounds, an attempt to predict the date for the Second Coming of Jesus. Some dim bulb had it all figured out—the Lord was returning in September 1975. My college classmates and I had discussions, because we had dreams about what we were going to try to accomplish for the kingdom of God, and we all felt the same way. Yes, we wanted Jesus to come, but we still had so many dreams about what we wanted to accomplish for his glory. That's healthy. That's completely healthy. So Paul was living in his *now*, but he was also embracing the *not yet*.

---

[56] Philippians 1:20-26, New International Version

[57] John 3:30, King James Version

If you're living in the now and you're not even thinking about the future, you're going to burn out now. If you're not doing anything now because you're just waiting for the future, you're missing the point, because God has a plan for you right now. Don't wait for something to change. *"For to me, to live is Christ..."* Not *Christian* but *Christ.* I identify with Jesus Christ. *"...to die is gain."* That's a great verse to describe what it means to be a follower of Jesus. I want to live so that people see Christ in me, and when I die everything will even get better. Paul doesn't say he wants to live a "Christian" life—he wants to live the CHRIST-life.

What's the difference? Well, I leave it to the brilliant mind and pen of the late C. S. Lewis to parse the words:

"People ask: 'Who are you, to lay down who is, and who is not a Christian?': or 'May not many a man who cannot believe these doctrines be far more truly a Christian, far closer to the spirit of Christ, than some who do?' Now this objection is in one sense very right, very charitable, very spiritual, very sensitive. It has every available quality except that of being useful. We simply cannot, without disaster, use language as these objectors want us to use it. I will try to make this clear by the history of another, and very much less important, word.

The word *gentleman* originally meant something recognizable; one who had a coat of arms and some landed property. When you called someone 'a gentleman' you were not paying him a compliment, but merely stating a fact. If you said he was not 'a gentleman' you were not insulting him, but giving information. There was no contradiction in saying that John was a liar and a gentleman; any more than there now is in saying that James is a fool and an M.A. But then there came people who said - so rightly, charitably, spiritually, sensitively, so anything but usefully - 'Ah but surely the important thing about a gentleman is not the coat of arms and the land, but the behavior? Surely he is the true gentleman who behaves as a gentleman should? Surely in that sense Edward is far more truly a gentleman than John?' They meant well. To be honorable and courteous and brave is of course a far better thing than to have a coat of arms. But it is not the same thing. Worse still, it is not a thing everyone will agree about. To call a man 'a gentleman' in this new, refined sense, becomes, in fact, not a way of giving information about him, but a way of praising him: to deny that he is "a gentleman" becomes simply a way of insulting him. When a word ceases to be a term of description and becomes merely a term of praise, it no longer tells you facts about the object: it only tells you about the speaker's attitude to that object. (A 'nice' meal only means a meal the speaker likes.) A gentleman, once it has been spiritualized and refined out of its old coarse, objective sense, means hardly more than a man whom the speaker likes. As a result, gentleman is now a useless word. We had lots of terms of approval already, so it was not needed for that use; on the other hand, if anyone (say, in a historical work) wants to use it in its old sense, he cannot do so without explanations. It has been spoiled for that purpose.

Now if once we allow people to start spiritualizing and refining, or as they might say 'deepening', the sense of the word Christian, it too will speedily become a useless word. In the first place, Christians themselves will never be able to apply it to anyone. It is not for us to say who, in the deepest sense, is or is not close to the spirit of Christ. We do not see into men's hearts. We cannot judge, and are indeed forbidden to judge. It would be wicked arrogance for us to say that any man is, or is not, a Christian in this refined sense. And obviously a word which we can never apply is not going to be a very useful word. As for the unbelievers, they will no doubt cheerfully use the word in the refined sense. It will become in their mouths simply a term of praise. In calling anyone a Christian they will mean that they think him a good man. But that way of using the word will be no enrichment of the language, for we already have the word good. Meanwhile, the word Christian will have been spoiled for any really useful purpose it might have served."[58]

He nailed it.

So did Paul.

---

[58] From the Preface to "Mere Christianity," by C. S. Lewis, 1947

Think on These Things

What does it mean to exalt Christ?

What do we mean by "now, and not yet?"

What is the Christ-life?

How has the term "Christian" been watered down?

READING:
Philippians 1:20-26
John 3:16-30
"Mere Christianity," by C. S. Lewis

CHAPTER TEN

Citizens of Joyland

The day our country was founded, a document was read. It was written by Thomas Jefferson, who had been tasked by the Continental Congress with putting down on paper the fruit of their recent debate and their decades-long journey toward national independence. Most Americans are familiar with some of the opening words. They talk about how human beings are "endowed by their Creator with certain unalienable rights, that among these are life, liberty and the pursuit of happiness."

Digging into the background of those words we learn that when Jefferson used the word "happiness," it was as a euphemism. Though we today might read it as "whatever makes someone happy," that's not quite what he meant. He was borrowing thoughts from a political philosopher who had written a hundred years earlier. His name was John Locke, and he wrote about the government's responsibility to protect citizens and their rights. Among those, Locke said, were "life, liberty, and the pursuit of *property*." Jefferson substituted the word "happiness," but he certainly knew that political "happiness" and the protection of the private property of citizens were related.[59]

All these years later, people still refer to America as a land of opportunity. A place to pursue dreams. As citizens of the republic, we have certain rights. They are protected. The idea of "citizenship" is old—dating back to the Greeks and Romans, tied to the concepts of popular democracy and republicanism (not the GOP, but the idea of a republic).

Roman citizenship was a big deal. No taxes—the conquered peoples paid those. Roman citizens had real rights when it came to due process. They didn't live in a democracy, but they had a measure of protection from the state.

Interestingly, outside of Rome, one of the places with a high concentration of Roman citizens in its population, was Philippi. It was called a "colony" and it was regarded as a mini-Rome. By the way, it was a favorite retirement destination for members of the Palace Guard. They'd get their big settlement for twenty years of service and could live tax-free. Nero didn't want a lot of retired soldiers in Rome in case there was a political uprising, so the retired military men were encouraged to move away. Many moved to Philippi. It was a great place to be a Roman citizen.

Paul loved to make the analogy about a believer's relationship with the Kingdom of God and Roman citizenship. He did it a couple of times in his letter, the first time in chapter one.

---

[59] See: "An Essay Concerning Human Understanding," by John Locke (1632-1704)

"Whatever happens, conduct yourselves in a manner worthy of the gospel of Christ. Then, whether I come and see you or only hear about you in my absence, I will know that you stand firm in the one Spirit, striving together as one for the faith of the gospel without being frightened in any way by those who oppose you. This is a sign to them that they will be destroyed, but that you will be saved—and that by God. For it has been granted to you on behalf of Christ not only to believe in him, but also to suffer for him, since you are going through the same struggle you saw I had, and now hear that I still have."[60]

The words *conduct* and *manner* are tied to the Greek concept of *politeuomai*—from the root word *polis*. That's the root of every English word having to do with *politics* or *policy*. It has to do with how people and nations are organized and function. He's basically saying, "Live like *citizens* of heaven. Live like you are heaven's representatives on earth so when people look at you they'll get a good idea of what heaven must be like."

In the book of Ephesians, he talked about the commonwealth. I love that word *commonwealth*. Are you familiar with it? There are four states in the United States of America that are actually described as *commonwealths*. Virginia is one. The others are Kentucky, Pennsylvania, and Massachusetts (and you thought it was called *The People's Republic of Massachusetts*).

What does the word *commonwealth* mean? It's in the words: common welfare, community. The idea of a commonwealth is as old as antiquity, even in Rome, even before that in the nation of Israel. It is a community of people looking out for each other—a

---

[60] Philippians 1:27-30, New International Version

community of people with common values. We're fellow citizens, citizens of the kingdom of God. What does this mean in practical terms?

First, we should be people of *conviction*. Choose conviction. Stand firm. You have to stand—for and against—if you're going to be a person of conviction. If all you're doing is standing *against* stuff, it's not right. It's an affirmative stance. You stand *for* something. You stand *for* Jesus. You stand *for* the gospel. You stand *for* the kingdom of God. When you're doing that, then you can stand against evil.

We are also to be people who practice *cooperation*. We choose to work with each other. Frankly, there were some in the church at Philippi who were having a hard time getting along with others. He told them, "Listen. You contend as one man. In one Spirit, cooperate with each other. Don't fight each other. Fight the good fight of faith. Get the gospel out to those who need it." One spirit. Unity. God loves that word. Unity does not mean *uniformity*. You don't have to be like each other. You have to *like* each other, but you don't have to *be* like each other. Unity doesn't always mean *unanimity*. But it does mean you agree on the big stuff.

We have to agree about Jesus. We have to agree that the Bible is the Word of God. We have to believe that you get saved by grace through faith plus nothing. We have to agree that Jesus is coming again literally. There are a number of things that are in a church's doctrinal statement. You do not have to agree with me that tea is better without sugar. I question your judgment if you don't. You're clearly wrong, but in the great national debate between sweet tea and unsweetened tea, we don't have to be unanimous.

What is it St. Augustine said? *"In essential things, unity; in nonessential things, liberty; in everything, charity."* Keep the main thing the main thing. Be unified. You hear words like *harmony* and *unity*. In music, you have melody and harmony. Melody drives the engine. You can have harmony, but if you don't have melody, something essential is missing. Melody is purpose, what drives it. It's the song you sing.

You can be in a group of people and have harmony, but you're not going anywhere if you don't have melody. Melody is unity. You're singing the same song. You're in the same key. If you're in the key of C, you can have the C and the A and the F, and you can have harmony, but if somebody throws an F sharp or a B flat in there, you're not in accord; you're in what is called *discord*.

Discord happens in groups when they're trying to sing the same song but someone is off-key, not singing the same note. In ministry, we want unity. The melody is the song of Jesus. We'll all bring our own harmony into it, as long as we stay in the same key, as long as we make sure the melody is the main thing.

Finally, we are to be people of *courage*. He said, *"without being frightened in any way by those who oppose you."* Don't be a person who's scared to death by those who oppose you. When you make a choice to follow Jesus and everything doesn't work out the way you think it should, just remember God has given you the gift to learn what it is like to be like Jesus.

There's a special kind of intimacy you can have with God when you're going through pain. He said, "I want you to have courage. Do not be afraid." Wow. Choose joy. Happiness comes and goes. Happiness happens, but you can choose joy, even if you don't feel like it. You choose it by faith, and God will kick it in supernaturally. You'll be able to say, as Paul did centuries ago, *"For to me, to live is Christ and to die is gain."*[61]

---

[61] Philippians 1:21, New International Version

Think on These Things

What does it mean to have "heavenly citizenship?"

What does unity mean?

What does unity NOT mean?

How do we develop healthy convictions?

READING:
Philippians 1:27-30
Ephesians 2:11-22

CHAPTER ELEVEN

Go Ahead, Make My Day

My mother was never happy when my brothers and I fought. I'm the oldest of three sons, and when we were kids my brother Greg (two years younger) and I tended to have our moments. All his fault, of course. Mom would often sigh, or shout, "Why can't you boys get along like David and Ricky Nelson, or Wally and the Beaver?" They were popular television brothers in the early 1960s. Never mind that we could recall several episodes where the TV bros *didn't* get along, sharing that fact to counter Mom's plea would have been an inconvenient truth.

It was only when I became a grandparent that I fully understood my mother's desire for sibling unity. I never really thought of it much when we were raising our three daughters, because moments when they weren't getting along were few and far between. Then came the grandsons—six of them (and one granddaughter). Sometimes they play together just wonderfully, and we'll post a nice photo on Facebook and caption it, "Look at these angels." Then it will all turn to, well, you know. They'll be hitting each other with iPads and all kinds of stuff. It's just the nature of things. That doesn't make me happy. It doesn't make my wife happy.

It's much more joyful when people we love get along with each other.

That was on Paul's mind when he wrote:

"Therefore, if you have any encouragement from being united with Christ, if any comfort from his love, if any common sharing in the Spirit, if any tenderness and compassion, then make my joy complete by being like-minded, having the same love, being one in spirit and of one mind."[62]

As Valentine's Day approached last year, I asked my wife, "What would like to do?" She said, "Do you know what I'd really like to do?"

"What?"

"Well, you know that place I took you on Father's Day a few years ago to see *The Great Escape* (the classic 1960s movie) on the big screen?"

"Sure," I replied, sensing danger (I may have heard scary music).

"Well, they're showing a movie *I* really like."

My first response was, "Good." Because we share no taste in movies whatsoever. "Sure! I'd be happy to. What movie is it?"

---

[62] Philippians 2:1-2, New International Version

Thinking it was going to be some sappy romantic comedy. Surely not *Patton* or *Tora, Tora, Tora*.

She said, "It's *The Princess Bride*"—a movie I actually liked (please don't tell anyone).

I paused, smiled, and then said, "As you wish."[63]

You had to be there.

When we went to see it, I suspect they had an original print of the film from 1987, none of that re-mastered stuff. Early on it started messing up. The sound was garbled, then the lip movements of the actors didn't match the soundtrack. Fortunately, we were surrounded by fans of the movie who knew every word of the dialogue by heart. It was amusing.

And a little scary.

A movie, as well as everything else in life, works better when things are *in sync*.

Nothing takes the wind out of our sails more than conflict—and the accompanying tension. Paul was aware of a particular conflict in the church at Philippi, one he would deal with later in his letter. For now, his message is: "Please make my day—put a smile on my face—get along with each other. Make my joy complete.

The indication is that joy is better when people in our lives are in sync.

---

[63] Wesley in "The Princess Bride," 1987

Paul lived vicariously. There was somewhat of a constructive co-dependent relationship Paul had with the people he'd influenced. What does it mean to be *like-minded*? It means to think and to say the *same thing*. Same love. Same spirit. Same mind. Same direction.

And same *pace*.

Sometimes a group of people—for example, a church—can be going in the right direction, but not moving in sync because of pacing. There have been times as a pastor when I have been way out in front, only to look back and notice that nobody was following. I've had to make adjustments.

There have also been times in my ministry when most have been in sync, and there were a few people setting their own pace for their own reasons. They were very energetic, and I could sense they felt I was moving too slow. But my pace was deliberate, as a leader I knew there were some who would burn out if things weren't paced correctly. I would try to convince the speedsters to stay with me and be patient, but they had their own agenda and perception of how the church should be functioning. It was almost like they were saying, "Well, how come you're so slow, Preacher? You must not be very spiritual."

This doesn't mean a vision is bad and that people shouldn't be passionate. It just simply means you have to follow that pace, because the person who is leading (this is true in any organization) is in a better position to understand the dynamics of the group as a whole. That's why the writer of the Book of Hebrews, when talking about leaders, suggests that some followers can cause grief, as opposed to joy.

"Obey those who rule over you, and be submissive, for they watch out for your souls, as those who must give account. Let them do so with joy and not with grief, for that would be unprofitable for you."[64]

We will all stand before the Lord one day—He will hold us accountable. Spiritual leaders will give an account of their sphere of influence. As a pastor, I will give an account about the local church ministry. Part of it will be difficult; part of it will be delightful. By the way, if you read that verse from the Book of Hebrews carefully, it indicates that being a good and supportive follower of a leader who is following the Lord is an act of *self-interest*.

Did you ever hear someone say, "That person gave me so much grief"? Where does that phrase come from? Grief comes when the joy is sucked out of you. Frankly, there are too many joy-suckers hanging around us. When one of them gets to me, I remember what the Lord told Joshua, *"Be strong and courageous."*[65]

The opposite of courage is not fear. The opposite of courage is *discouragement*. You don't have to be filled with fear; you just have to have the wind knocked out of you. If you're a follower, be the kind of follower you would want if you were leading. If you're a leader, be the kind of leader you'd want to follow. Work hard to be in sync. Move at the same pace. Move in the same direction. When a church can do that, when a group can do that, when a family can do that, when a community can do that, great things can happen.

---

64 Hebrews 13:17, New King James Version

65 Joshua 1:6, New International Version

Any organization is more effective and efficient when people are in sync. Otherwise there will be chaos and disorder.

"Do nothing out of selfish ambition or vain conceit. Rather, in humility value others above yourselves, not looking to your own interests but each of you to the interests of the others. In your relationships with one another, have the same mindset as Christ Jesus."[66]

Years after I finished Bible college and seminary, I decided to go back to school to earn secular degrees in history and political science. Part of this involved the study of political philosophy. I had to read a lot of the old classics—toe-tappers by writers like Hobbes, Locke, Hume, Aristotle and Plato.

Aristotle lived about 400 years before Paul, but the future apostle's education included familiarity with the Greek philosopher's writings—including one treatise called, simply, *Politics*. When Paul used the word *eritheía* ("strife" or "selfish ambition") in his letter to his friends in Philippi, he was likely recalling how Aristotle used it. It literally meant *someone campaigning unfairly or unethically for a position*, for an opinion, or for an office. Aristotle used it in the context of politics. Paul used that same word to describe strife in the church.

Sometimes people in the church start "campaigning" and work on others to win loyalties and followers. They may not be bad people, but they go about things all wrong and are driven by pride. They begin to work on people and draw people to them like they're campaigning for an office or trying to gather a following. Church

---

66 Philippians 2:3-4, New International Version

members should beware of the follower or followers who aren't in sync with a leader's vision.

It's a joyful thing to live in sync.

Think on These Things

Have I ever sowed discord in a church or small group?

Why did reports of conflict at Philippi bother Paul so much?

Why is complaining a sin?

How does murmuring hinder the work and will of God?

Does spiritual growth make me immune from emotional struggles?

READING:
Philippians 2:1-4
Psalm 133
James 3:13-18
I Corinthians 3:1-9

CHAPTER TWELVE

Think Like Jesus

Albert Einstein was pretty smart. But I can't think like him. I can, however, think like Jesus. In fact, it's pretty much a commandment.

"Your attitude should be the same as that of Christ Jesus."[67]

My mother never pulled that one on us—it might have worked.

What does it mean to have the mindset of Christ Jesus? Think like Jesus. You want to be like Jesus? I think everyone ought to. Well, this is a gateway into one of the most awesome, profound, deep, awe-inspiring passages of Scripture dealing with Christ's mission on the earth.

"Who, being in very nature God, did not consider equality with God something to be used to his own advantage; rather, he made himself nothing by taking the very nature of a servant, being made

---

67 Philippians 2:5, New International Version

in human likeness. And being found in appearance as a man, he humbled himself by becoming obedient to death—even death on a cross! Therefore God exalted him to the highest place and gave him the name that is above every name, that at the name of Jesus every knee should bow, in heaven and on earth and under the earth, and every tongue acknowledge that Jesus Christ is Lord, to the glory of God the Father.[68]

To think like Jesus, we have to be willing to *lay aside our rights*. It doesn't mean we don't have rights. We do. So did Jesus. But there are times in life when it's best not to insist on them. When you have children, you start laying aside your rights to sleep, to complete autonomy over your money. That's the mark of maturity. Let me just say another thing. When you're in the grandparent generation (as I am), you also have to learn to sacrifice some rights.

All across America, churches are trying to change to make sure they don't lose the younger generation, and some of the people fighting it the most are older people. They're being very selfish and childish. They're willing to let a church die rather than lose some of their "rights" and preferences. But then there some older people who think differently—they're thinking like Jesus. They're willing to give up a few preferences in order to save a younger generation.

As we get older, we should grow more joyful, not more grumpy. The key is to be mature by laying aside our rights. The right to tell everyone what we think and what they should be doing. That really doesn't work anyway.

---

68 Philippians 2:6-11, New International Version

To think like Jesus, we must *follow his example of humility.*

The most important thing to learn about humility is that we should never assume that humbling us is something God does. He can, of course, and He does quite often. But it is really plan "B." God humbles those who refuse to humble *themselves* before him. It is a corrective measure. It's always preferred that we self-correct, and when it comes to the virtue of humility, that means we must take the initiative.

"So humble yourselves before God. Resist the devil, and he will flee from you. Come close to God, and God will come close to you. Wash your hands, you sinners; purify your hearts, for your loyalty is divided between God and the world. Let there be tears for what you have done. Let there be sorrow and deep grief. Let there be sadness instead of laughter, and gloom instead of joy. Humble yourselves before the Lord, and he will lift you up in honor."[69]

The idea is that we should not be filling our lives with empty things, but rather we should empty ourselves so God can fill us with His power and purpose and lift us up.

Jesus also demonstrated the most defining aspect of true humility—He was *obedient.* He was obedient to the point of death. He was obedient throughout the ordeal of the cross. He was obedient no matter what.

Understanding the cross is crucial to our experience of profound joy. The very word *crucial* is based on the cross. In fact, "cross" is the root of our English words *crucial, crux,* and *crucible.* The

---

[69] James 4:7-10, New Living Translation

words speak of something vital—even central—as well as painful. I find this fascinating. In fact, long before Jesus went to the cross to die for our sins, He talked about the cross as a concept.

"Then Jesus said to his disciples, 'If any of you wants to be my follower, you must give up your own way, take up your cross, and follow me.'"[70]

We tend to interpret His admonition with the clarity of historical hindsight—through His cross, where He suffered and died. But when we look closer, it's clear that no one had any reason at that point in His ministry to associate the cross as a method of capital punishment with Him. The concept of a cross was known. It was about humiliation and pain. Crucifixion was a Roman mode of punishment for criminal offenders. It was designed to be a public ordeal. And part of the ordeal was that the condemned person had to carry his own cross to the place of crucifixion.

It would be like bringing your own rope to the hanging. Or, as my grandmother used to request when I had misbehaved (most likely, she had just misunderstood), "David, you go out to that tree in the yard and cut a switch." I had to find the tool with which I'd be punished and then transport it back to the person determined to use it. I guess it was a way to carry my own cross. She'd add, "And you think about what you've done, young man."

The cross was a process.

A painful process.

---

[70] Matthew 16:24, New Living Translation

When Paul told the believers at Philippi that the cross was the ultimate example of our Lord's obedience, he was speaking of the cross not only as something Jesus went *to*, but also something He went *through*. So it must be with us—His professed followers. The cross is not just a destination—it's a *journey*. A journey of difficulty. A *crucible*.

Pain is never pleasant. Suffering is never satisfying. It is, however, *purifying*, *clarifying*, and, in its own way, *empowering*. Humility precedes honor. It's a vital prelude. The promise from God is that if we humble ourselves, He will lift us up. So, if we want to move up, we must first aim low.

Most of the great victories in our lives take time. Before we get to the pinnacle, we must carry our cross. Glory is deferred. Victory is delayed. Jesus had to go to the cross to get the victory. It's like the verse in the book of Hebrews. He is *"the author and finisher of our faith, who for the joy that was set before Him endured the cross."*[71]

He was obedient because He knew the ultimate outcome.

I witnessed the births of all three of my daughters, one in Michigan; one in Texas; and one in Illinois. Wonderful moments, from my vantage point. But it was clear to me that there were some moments during that childbirth process when my wife seemed to be in some discomfort. I have great observational skills. It was painful. Why did she do it? Better question: why would she do it again? Because she knew joy was waiting on the other side of the pain—and that helped her get through it.

---

[71] Hebrews 12:2, King James Version

Our capacity to handle pain and suffering is directly related to our confidence in a compelling outcome.

When we humble ourselves in the sight of the Lord, there will come a time when God will reach down and say, "Okay, you've spent enough time in your timeout. I'm going to pick you up and put you on a rock and give you an opportunity you never thought you would have."

"Humble yourselves in the sight of the Lord, and he shall lift you up." In that word *and*, we don't know how long that takes. It doesn't mean as soon as you humble yourself, *Boom! Boom!* You're up. It could be a year. It could be a month. It could be a week. It could be a day. It could be ten years.

Bow down and wait.

Think on These Things

How did Jesus lay aside his rights?

How does humility lead to exaltation?

What does it mean to bear the cross?

How can suffering HELP us?

> **READING:**
> Philippians 2:5-11
> James 4:7-10
> Hebrews 12:1-3

CHAPTER THIRTEEN

Humble Like Jesus

What God means by humility—complete humility—is not some kind of half-measure. It's total submission. And we have a powerful example, one that cannot be denied or explained away.

"He made himself nothing by taking the very nature of a servant, being made in human likeness. And being found in appearance as a man, he humbled himself by becoming obedient to death—even death on a cross!"[72]

That's powerful! All right. What was Christ's example? I see three things.

Jesus laid aside his rights.

I remember the time I heard Jerry Falwell talk about this. He was once a stage with Billy Graham and there was a Christian rap-artist

---

[72] Philippians 2:8, New International Version

doing his thing. Certainly, the presentation was not the usual cup of tea for Billy or Jerry. It was not George Beverly Shea, or even Ethel Waters. Graham said to Falwell, "What do you think of this?"

"Oh, I don't know, he is a fine young man," Jerry replied.

"Well, I imagine what he is talking about is good," Billy said.

"Yeah. It's fine," Jerry added.

You'd never see them enjoying it, but they enjoyed seeing a new generation of people with their own methodology bring people to Jesus Christ. These wise men knew something about yielding their rights.

I'm in my 60s, and I'll start talking to my much-younger staff members about something from the 1960s, and their eyes will glaze over like. Many of my cultural references are from black-and-white TV. They don't even know what that means. I still fight every Christmas for Christmas vespers. I love Christmas vespers. It's an evening service at Christmas, but they vote it down. One year we're going to have it. It's going to be called *Vespers*. You say, "I don't even know what that means." I don't either. I just like the word—*vespers*.

Jesus deliberately humbled himself.

In theology, the whole Philippians chapter two passage is called the *kenosis*. It comes from the Greek idea of emptying something. Jesus emptied himself as he humbled himself. It's the same Greek word similarly used and translated as *vainglory*. *Vain* means empty. The idea is that we shouldn't fill our lives with empty things, we should empty our lives of anything that is not consistent with Jesus. He obeyed even to the death of the cross. Is there a line you will not cross? Is there something you will not do? "I just don't do that." Not Jesus.

Jesus was ultimately exalted.

It's the great point. *"Therefore, God exalted him and gave him the name that is above every name, that at the name of Jesus every knee should bow."* In other words, glory is a deferred experience. All the great victories in our lives (or at least most of them) will take time. Before we get to that pinnacle, there may be some humbling that happens first. It's deferred. It comes later.

Jesus had to go to and through the cross to get the victory. It's like the verse in the book of Hebrews. He is, *"the author and finisher of our faith, who for the joy that was set before Him endured the cross."*[73] He had something joyful on his mind. That's how he got through it. How did he become obedient? He knew the outcome. He knew the result. He knew what was going to happen.

When you humble yourself in the sight of the Lord, there will come a time when God will reach down. You may think it's never going to happen. God has abandoned you. God will reach down and say, "Okay, you've spent enough time in your time-out. I'm going to

---

[73] Hebrews 12:2, New International Version

pick you up and put you on a rock and give you an opportunity you never thought you would have."

The Bible says, *"Humble yourselves in the sight of the Lord, and he shall lift you up."* We don't know how long that "and" takes. It doesn't mean as soon as you humble yourself, *Boom! Boom!* You're up. It could be a year. It could be a month. It could be a week. It could be a day. It could be ten years. Whatever the issue might be, you humble yourself, and you wait there. Like David said, "I humbled myself. I was in a pit. It was like miry clay. Then the Lord heard me and reached down and put me on a solid rock."[74]

Then you'll be exalted.

"And let us not be weary in well doing: for in due season we shall reap, if we faint not."[75]

---

[74] Psalm 40:1-3, New International Version

[75] Galatians 6:9, King James Version

Think on These Things

How do we lay aside our rights, generationally?

How does service relate to suffering?

What is the key to enduring hardship?

What is the "kenosis?"

READING:
Philippians 2:1-18
Psalm 40:1-3
I Corinthians 15:51-58
Galatians 6:1-9

CHAPTER FOURTEEN

Living Inside Out

I've described the basic difference between happiness and joy—the latter being the better deal. One way of saying it is this: Happiness is driven by something on the outside—people, circumstances, events, etc.—whereas joy is all about what's going on *inside* us.

Most people go through life being driven by stuff on the outside.

Authentic followers of Jesus learn the great truth that real living, the kind that Jesus described as abundant living,[76] requires us to learn to live *inside out.*

"Therefore, my dear friends, as you have always obeyed—not only in my presence, but now much more in my absence continue to work out your salvation with fear and trembling."[77]

It doesn't mean that we must work to get saved. He is saying God has saved you, He has done something in you, so live accordingly.

---

[76] John 10:10, King James Version

[77] Philippians 2:12, New International Version

The next verse says, *"for it is God who works in you to will and to act in order to fulfill his good purpose."*[78] What he is saying is, "Work it out." In other words, what's going on inside you, don't hold it there. Let it work out. Let it become the dominant force in your life.

And it may surprise you where this kind of living begins.

"Do everything without grumbling or arguing, so that you may become blameless and pure, children of God without fault in a warped and crooked generation."[79]

Wait, what? Surely there are societal, cultural, and ecclesiastical ills that are worse than whining. Well, yes and no. Of course, there are sins that reach the level of abomination. But there are also what we might call "slippery slope" sins. Just as when Paul wrote to the Romans about how the failure to be thankful was at the root of so many greater evils, so it is with our tendency to gripe and complain. Why? Because once we go down that road, we have taken our eyes off God, His grace, and His plan, and are sliding into the realm of the flesh.

If you're trying to be a witness to the world and all you do is complain about everything at work, in your neighborhood, or at home, you're never going to be effective. You're sending mixed signals. On the other hand, if people see us putting up with stuff without complaint because Jesus never complained, they're going to notice that.

---

[78] Philippians 2:13, New International Version

[79] Philippians 2:14, New International Version

Paul wrote to the Corinthians about fornication, idolatry, murmuring, and complaining all at the same level.[80] In my thinking, idolatry and fornication seem more wicked than giving way to frustration and complaining about something. But God sees it differently. If you're a constant critic and complaining about everything in life, whether in the church or outside the church, He says you have to do *all things* without murmuring and disputing. Don't complain. Don't be argumentative.

I remember many years ago when I was pastoring in New York, my first year there, there was a guy who had been very involved in the church. He didn't like anything I did, any change I made. Part of it was because he was very close to my predecessor. I understood that, so I gave him a lot of rope. I spent a lot of time with the guy. He happened to live four or five doors down from us, so we'd talk. We'd go out for walks. We'd have coffee. He always had a problem. "Well, you know, you're not doing it like Pastor So-and-So did it." I'd reply, "I'm not him. He is a great man. I honor what he did." Every time I thought I had him talked off the ledge ("Oh, I get it, Preacher. You're right. That makes perfect sense. Okay, I've got your back"), a few days later, he was back with another complaint. No matter what, he just kept arguing and arguing.

Have you ever been around somebody like that? You just can't convince them, because they're never going to let go. They're like a dog with a bone? That's the person who is an arguer and a complainer. That's the antithesis of being Christ like.

If you've never committed adultery, you've never stolen a dime, you've never been drunk, you've never lied, you've never cheated,

---

[80] See: I Corinthians 10:1-13

and you think you're a good Christian, but all you do is sit around and complain and gripe, then you have no real testimony. He says you have to be "*blameless and pure, children of God without fault in a warped and crooked generation, in which you shine like stars in the universe.*"[81]

Paul was living and writing that in the first century. Do we not still live in a crooked world? What's our role? "Our role is to beat them up." No. Our role is to shine among them like stars in the sky. The Bible indicates that we actually function best against a dark sky. You go out here at night in an area where there's a lot of light, and you don't see all the stars that are there. But when it's really dark, you get away from civilization, you see them fill the sky. Yes, the world is an evil place. Yes, everything is turned upside down. Yes, biblical values are ignored in secular society. But we are called to counter these things.

The darker the world is out there, the brighter we can be for Jesus. Turn it around and use it to the advantage of the kingdom of God. *"As you hold firmly to the word of life. And then I will be able to boast on the day of Christ that I did not run or labor in vain."*[82]

Live inside out. Let that which is working in you (God who is working in you) come out through your words, through your actions, through your body language, through your living in sync with the people of God, through your living to follow the Lord Jesus' example. Work it out. Live it out.

---

[81] Philippians 2:15, New International Version

[82] Philippians 2:16, New International Version

A while back, I helped an author publish a biography of his preacher-grandfather. He was a beloved figure, in fact, one of my heroes in life. He passed away at an elderly age in 2002. I was privileged to study what's called *Pastoral Theology* under him. In other words, he got up and talked about what pastors do. It was the best class I ever had. It was just very practical.

He told a lot of great stories about his life. At one time, he pastored the largest church in the state of Missouri. He told us great stories, but there is one he never told us. I read it in the author's manuscript. He was called to a great church in 1941 just before World War II started, and then he left in 1963. I was always puzzled as to why he left and took another church in Florida. I learned the rest of the story. After he had been there 22 years, there was a problem. A few years earlier, he had hired somebody who was very talented, a very gifted person, but this person undermined him at every turn. He drew disciples after himself. By this time, this pastor's son was a Bible college grad, and he was the youth pastor in the church. He began to catch wind of it. All the undermining was, of course, done in the shadows and with whispers—that's the methodology of anything devilish.

Finally, the old pastor decided to confront the problem and deal with it, thinking he could. The guy who was causing this said, "Yeah, I guess I'll move on." He said, "Okay." Then the outgoing conspirator asked, "Can I just say goodbye to the church on Sunday?" The gracious pastor said, "Sure." And the guy got up on the Sunday following. Instead of just saying, "Goodbye. It's been a pleasure," he decided to talk about all the things that were wrong with the church and the pastor and things he had been saying in private. It was devastating to this pastor. He was a wonderful man.

The church was thrown into crisis and confusion. They had a meeting. Long story short, 500 people left the church because of the damage done by the associate.

A very sad story. A church can't grow when it's driven by complaint. In fact, no one can grow when driven by complaint.

Growth comes—and with it joy—when we learn to live *inside out*.

Think on These Things

What does it mean to live "inside out?"

What does God do "in" us?

This complaining wrong?

How does complaining short-circuit joy?

How can we be lights in the world?

READING:
Philippians 2:12-16
I Corinthians 10:1-13
John 10:1-10

CHAPTER FIFTEEN

Incarnational Ministry: Timothy

Paul said, *"For to me, to live is Christ."* That's the ultimate ideal. *"and to die is gain."* Christ coming to the world was a matter of *incarnation*—which means "clothed with flesh." We can use it in the theological sense, as in the idea that Jesus was God in the flesh, or we can describe something as being the ultimate embodiment or representation.

For example, Ted Williams was the incarnation of the greatest hitter in baseball.

God became man. *"And the Word was made flesh, and dwelt amongst us, (and we beheld his glory, the glory as of the only begotten of the Father,) full of grace and truth,"* as the Apostle John wrote.[83] As we explore the idea of choosing joy, we find people in the pages of scripture who were, in a very real sense, the embodiment of this virtue—the ministry of incarnation.

---

83 John 1:14, King James Version

What is the *ministry* of incarnation? It's when we seek to embody and express the Word of God that's at work in us. Hebrews 4:12: *"For the word of God is quick, and powerful, and sharper than any two-edged sword, piercing even to the dividing asunder of soul and spirit, and of the joints and marrow, and is a discerner of the thoughts and intents of the heart."*[84] The Word gets inside us—under our skin. Paul told the Thessalonians, *"…the word…which is effectually at work in you who believe…."*[85]

The Word of God goes to work *in* us.

"Therefore, my dear friends, as you have obeyed—not only in my presence, but now much more in my absence—continue to work out your salvation with fear and trembling. For it is God who works in you to will and to act according to his good purpose."[86]

In another place, Paul described Christ-followers as jars of clay. We are human, but we have a treasure in an earthen vessel.[87] The goal is to have the treasure magnified. The Word was made flesh in the classic sense in Jesus, but every one of us who knows Christ is called to let the Word be made flesh in us. It's not only the words we say that bear witness to Jesus, but that the lives we live are to demonstrate his power.

Paul wrote about two men who were poster children for incarnational ministry—Timothy and Epaphroditus.

---

[84] Hebrews 4:12, King James Version

[85] I Thessalonians 2:13, King James Version

[86] Philippians 2:12-13, New International Version

[87] II Corinthians 4:7, New International Version

"I hope in the Lord Jesus to send Timothy to you soon, that I also may be cheered when I receive news about you. I have no one else like him, who will show genuine concern for your welfare. For everyone looks out for their own interests, not those of Jesus Christ. But you know that Timothy has proved himself, because as a son with his father he has served with me in the work of the gospel. I hope, therefore, to send him as soon as I see how things go with me."[88]

We first met Timothy as young man in the Book of Acts. He was born in Lystra. His mother's name was Eunice, and his grandmother was Lois—Jewish women. His father was Greek. He apparently was already off the scene, likely had passed away. Eunice was a single mom. Timothy was converted as a child and grew to become a co-laborer with Paul. He was around when Paul wrote Colossians, 2 Corinthians, Ephesians, Philippians, and there are two epistles in scripture addressed directly to him. He was like a son to Paul. Theirs was a strong relationship. Paul called him a faithful helper.

The practice of prevailing joy includes deciding to be helpful to others in tangible ways. The first mark Paul talks about with Timothy in this is…

He was a sincere person.

His sincerity was noteworthy. Paul described Timothy as a rare breed—a unique treasure. In other words, he was looking for someone to send back to report to the church at Philippi, but

---

[88] Philippians 2:19-23, New International Version

nobody wanted to go. So Timothy stepped up. He was willing to do what others found distasteful or inconvenient. Why? Because he was sincerely and genuinely concerned about others.

He had kingdom priorities.

He had his priorities right. What does it say? A statement, a fact, that's a little hard to read about ourselves. *"For everyone looks out for their own interests, not those of Jesus Christ."* Now this may sound like a harsh statement, but I think he is stating a truth. We live our lives according to self-interest, and much (not all) of what we do in the spiritual realm is too-often dictated by self-interest. When I made my decision on May 12, 1968, to open my heart to Jesus, sure, it was about Jesus, but it was also a decision I made out of self-interest. I wanted the gift of eternal life. I did not want to be separated from God. Self-interest is not all bad. We're to love our neighbor as ourselves. There's a place for it.

When Paul says, *"Husbands, love your wives, as Christ loved the church,"* he also says, *"For no man ever hated his own flesh; but nourishes and cherishes it."*[89] It's in our best self-interest to walk according to God's plan for our lives. Do you want to live a better life? Do you want to have a safer life, a happier life, a more joyful life? Live according to the Word of God. Follow the will of God for your life. It's the best decision you can make. It's a very selfish decision, but it's right. Often, however, we let that self-interest drive how we pick and choose the things we will do. Timothy wasn't like that. He did what needed to be done. Most of us will pick and choose what we like. We like aspects of *this*. We like

---
89 Ephesians 5:22, New International Version

aspects of *that*. But not all of us (some are rare, like Timothy) do what we need to do to get the job done.

If you've worked around people for any length of time, or you've ever supervised a group of people, you know there are people who get stuff done, and there are people who never seem to get anything done. They're good at certain things, but others they don't want to touch.

In fact, everyone looks out for their own interest. He is not saying we're ever going to change that. We're always going to be self-interested, but he says Timothy steps up. I think part of this is a component of spiritual maturity. Timothy was under the influence of Paul who was obviously a deeply committed person himself.

Timothy was commended as a faithful helper because he was living proof of some valuable things. *"Because as a son with his father he has served with me in the work of the gospel."* They had that close relationship I spoke of. *"I hope, therefore, to send him as soon as I see how things go with me. And I am confident in the Lord that I myself will come soon."*

He was living proof. This is really important. God has stuff for us to do, but the process of proving is very important. Timothy proved himself. This was important to Paul, because he could be a tough guy. Remember the story of John Mark, Barnabas' relative, who was with him? Then he quit and went back home. Then later Barnabas said, "Let's bring him along because he has a lot of talent." Paul said, "No way. The guy is a loser. He quit." Barnabas and Paul fought really hard. They split up. Paul was hard-nosed. So when he described Timothy as having proved himself, that was high apostolic praise indeed.

Some of the greatest teachers I had growing up were also the strictest. In fact, the ones I admire the most were the strictest. They were hard to please.

This is not just for young people. It's for anybody. If you think things are going too slow in your life for God... I'm not just talking about in the church. I'm talking out *there*. You've been praying for an opportunity. Let me ask you a question. Is God waiting for you to prove yourself? Prove yourself faithful where you are right now. Be faithful in little and God may give you greater opportunities.

When God was choosing a new king, he sent Samuel to Bethlehem. He lined up Jesse's sons. They were a good-looking bunch of guys. But the baby of the family wasn't in the line-up. David (the youngest) was out in the field with the sheep. But he was the Lord's chosen one. Samuel anointed David, the little boy, the youngest brother, as the new king for Israel. It was a powerful, heady moment.

Then what?

Then the father said, "Okay, David. That was cool, wasn't it? Now get back out there to those sheep." David didn't say, "Whoa, Dad. You're talking to the king. I'm the king!" No. David went back out there and took care of the sheep for however long because the best place of preparation for what God has for you tomorrow and the next day and the next day and the next year is to be faithful to what he gives you *today*. Don't think, "Well, this is not worth my time." It *is* worth your time. Be faithful.

Think on These Things

Think about people who seem to embody certain qualities.

What does "incarnation" mean?

What virtues did Timothy embody?

How do we balance care for others with legitimate self-interest?

What are Kingdom priorities?

READING:
Philippians 2:12-23
I Thessalonians 2:10-13
John 1:1-14
Hebrews 4:12

CHAPTER SIXTEEN

Incarnational Ministry: Epaphroditus

Epaphroditus was in the church at Philippi, but he was not converted when Paul and company came to town. He was probably led to faith in Christ by one of the original members. We don't know a lot about him.

"But I think it is necessary to send back to you Epaphroditus, my brother, co-worker and fellow soldier, who is also your messenger, whom you sent to take care of my needs."[90]

One of the interesting features of Paul's first imprisonment in Rome was that he was responsible to provide funds for his domestic expenses, including the rental of his quarters. Can you imagine that? What a system, right? The church at Philippi heard about this and they raised some funds.

All they needed was a courier.

---

90 Philippians 2:25, New International Version

In spite of their collective generosity, there weren't likely a lot of volunteers for this task. It involved lengthy, difficult, and even down-right dangerous, travel. Then, once in Rome, it involved a public commitment to a man who was, after all, a prisoner of the state. The courier could possibly face his own troubles with the authorities.

It was a job for someone willing to put everything at risk.

Epaphroditus was the man for the job. We don't know much about him. He stepped out of obscurity for his own brief "fifteen minutes of fame." He's not a major player in church history, his is a minor role—a supporting role. But how he handled the trust of his Philippian brethren, and his experience while in Rome, mark him as a remarkable man. Paul describes him as a "messenger" of the faraway church, the Greek word being the same as for the word "apostle"—which literally means "one who is sent." Just as Paul was an apostle sent by God, Epaphroditus was an apostle sent by the church at Philippi.

After his arduous journey and welcomed arrival in Rome, Epaphroditus prolonged his stay and grew close to Paul. Paul referred to him as "my brother," and then he called him a "co-worker" and "fellow soldier." He ministered to Paul. He says, "He came to take care of my needs." Those four words "care of my needs" are translated in other translations "minister to my needs." That's because the word is very unique. In fact, the only time it's ever used in the word-for-word translations in the English Bible is in this passage. It's not a word usually used. It is different from the most common "servant" words (*diakonos*=deacon; *doulos*=servant/slave). This is something else.

It has to do with something more, well, *official*.

The Benefactor

A little background here. When my wife was growing up, her family lived for several years in Corning, New York, where her mother also grew up. It's a beautiful little town. They lived in a little house (she and her four siblings, her parents). Her dad worked at a local factory. They went to a good church there. In their neighborhood, all the houses were built very close together. Their house was probably the smallest on the block. I've seen it. I can't imagine how they raised so many kids there.

Just a block away, on this street filled with small houses, there stood a mansion. A very large, very grand, home. Big and beautiful. It's still there. The first time I saw it, Karen told me that when they were kids, it was owned by a family named Houghton, the founders of the famous *Corning Glass Works*. She said, "We would go over to that house and knock on the door. Maybe a maid or somebody would come to the door. They had a big trampoline out in the yard. They'd let the little kids in the neighborhood come and bounce around on that trampoline." She remembers doing that with her brothers and friends in the neighborhood. The Houghton family and others did a lot for their community.

More than a hundred years earlier, a young boy named Andy lived in Pennsylvania. He had a neighbor whose name was Colonel James Anderson. Anderson had been in the War of 1812. He took a liking to the young boys in the neighborhood, especially those who were willing to work hard and earn their keep. He had a large personal library and decided to share it with boys like Andy.

That is how young Andrew Carnegie grew to love books and learn a lot about life. Eventually, Carnegie became one of the richest people in the world. Later in life, as he began to face his own mortality and with thoughts about his legacy, he decided he wanted to be a giver. History tells us he gave about 90 percent of his fortune away. We still have his *National Endowment for the Arts* today. There's a university called *Carnegie Mellon.*

But Carnegie did something else, something rooted in his own childhood experience. He funded a vast system of public libraries across the country. There are 2,000 private, public, and academic libraries in the United States of America that were founded and completely funded by Andrew Carnegie. When I lived and pastored in Ohio, the library in that town was a Carnegie library. When I pastored in Illinois, the library was a Carnegie creation.

He was what we call a *benefactor*, someone who had been blessed who gave something back.

That's Epaphroditus. The word used for *minister* (*leitourgós*) goes back to the Greeks when they had the city-states. Athens was a city-state. Sparta was a city-state. They all had their own armies. There were people who were proud of their city-state. Rather than use tax money to do certain things, they would endow things like the arts. Some even paid for the army. They'd pay for education. They were *benefactors*. Paul uses that word to describe Epaphroditus. He came and ministered. He came to be a benefactor. It may be that the offering that was raised in Philippi included a significant amount of his own money. He was likely a very successful, probably wealthy, man.

The lesson should be obvious. We have all been blessed by God, but not so we can just smile and say, "Thank you, Jesus." Every blessing God has given you or given me, he has given us on loan so we can pay it forward to someone else. God never intended for us to be reservoirs, holding it all in. God intended for us to be rivers, letting it flow through. You'll be amazed what God will give you if you don't let much of it stick. Epaphroditus was a benefactor. He blessed. So should we. We should make the choice to rejoice through generosity.

The Risk Taker

The very name Epaphroditus gives us a clue about the man. He was probably a young adult when he came to faith in Christ. The indication is that his parents weren't believers, at least not when he was born. His name was fairly common in the day. It was tied to a Greek "goddess" by the name of Aphrodite. She was known as the goddess of love—but also the goddess of luck or chance.

In the musical, *Guys and Dolls,* when they're singing, *"Luck be a lady tonight,"* it's a saying that hearkens back to that goddess of luck. Back then, when people were playing games of chance, and they'd throw the dice. If they really wanted add a word of "encouragement" to the dice, they'd cry out "Okay, Epaphroditus!" The name was synonymous with, "Good luck!"

No Christian parent would attach that name to a newborn son. It was pagan. Paul saw the name as prophetically appropriate. He says, *"For he longs for all of you and is distressed because you heard he was ill."* He wasn't bothered that he was ill. He heard that they were worried about him, and that fact bothered him.

"Indeed, he was ill, and almost died. But God had mercy on him, and not on him only but also on me, to spare me sorrow upon sorrow. Therefore, I am all the more eager to send him, so that when you see him again you may be glad and I may have less anxiety. So then, welcome him in the Lord with great joy, and honor people like him, because he almost died for the work of Christ. He risked his life to make up for the help you yourselves could not give me."[91]

The word *risk* is very, very interesting. *"He risked his life."* He almost died. Just the fact that he made the journey to Rome was a risk. Paul was in a Roman prison under Nero. The charge was sedition. That's why a lot of people didn't hang out with Paul. Guilt by association. It was a risk even to associate yourself with somebody like this, but Epaphroditus did. *"He risked his life to make up for the help you yourselves could not give me."*

A righteous risk-taker.

The word *risk* comes from a particular Greek word—*parabouleúomai*. Years later, long after this epistle began to circulate, there was a group that took that word and made it the title of a movement called the *Parabalani*. Basically, they wanted to be like Epaphroditus. They were the special ops Christians, the SEAL Team Six Christians, who would go into dangerous situations, maybe facing illness, peril, or risk in order to advance the cause of Jesus Christ. One of the greatest examples of their work came a couple hundred years later.

---

[91] Philippians 2:26-27, New International Version

The year was 252 AD. In the city of Carthage, North Africa, there was a deadly plague killing people by the thousands. People were afraid to go near the dead bodies, so the diseased remains were not being buried, compounding the malady. The bishop of Carthage, a man named Cyprian, called out the *Parabalani*. They came and buried those bodies and they tended to the sick, helping to defeat the plague. They were the risk takers.

We might say it this way about Epaphroditus: he was *all in*. He didn't worry about the danger to himself. He didn't worry about what it meant. If it was something the Lord and the work needed, he did his part to get it done. These days, there is no group called the *Parabalani*, but I think about this. I wonder how much we risk, how much convenience we're willing to do without, how much comfort we're willing to reject, how much misunderstanding we're willing to accept, how many collateral consequences for taking a stand for Jesus we're willing to absorb.

Paul said of Epaphroditus: *"Honor men like him."*[92]

Indeed.

A while back, a missionary friend visited our church. We raised some money for his various missionary enterprises in Belgium and Cote d'Ivoire (Ivory Coast). He talked about the early days in his ministry. There were death threats, people coming at him with guns. I was sitting on the front row and thinking, "This is my college classmate, and he has really experienced those things!" You know, I've had people write me an angry email and not sign it, but

---

92 Philippians 2:29, New International Version

no one has ever come at me with a gun. I'm like a sissy boy compared to him.

American Christians may not be in physical danger, but some people in the world face such things every day. There are people operating in the shadow of ISIS right now for the cause of Jesus Christ. Do you realize many times missionaries on the foreign field are targets, not only of persecution but of potential death? Would you be willing to do that if God called you to do it?

You might think, "Well, I'd like to think I would." But, if you're not doing much for Jesus right now, you probably wouldn't. If you're not willing to live for him, you wouldn't be willing to die for him. That's hard to take, I know, but it's true. Paul raised up Timothy and Epaphroditus as examples of *incarnational* ministry.

Think on These Things

What is a benefactor, and how does this relate to God's work?

How was Epaphroditus a risk-taker?

And why did it matter?

Who were the *parabalani*?

How are people in harm's way in our age as they serve the Lord?

READING:
Philippians 2:25-29
Galatians 2:20
II Corinthians 9:6-15

CHAPTER SEVENTEEN

Dogs & Dung

We can make the choice to rejoice even in the midst of grief. We can choose joy while experiencing great pain. We can experience rejection and yet choose joy, not through positive thinking or pop psychology, but because the power of God is available to us. We can activate that power and choose joy in any moment—by faith. The joy of the Lord can indeed become our strength in such moments.

Now moving into the third chapter of Paul's letter, he says, *"Further, my brothers and sisters, rejoice in the Lord!"* I've told you when you see that phrase, it's another way of saying, "Choose joy!" *"It is no trouble for me to write the same things to you again, and it is a safeguard for you."*[93] It's like he is saying, "I've been repeating myself over and over and over again."

Why do people repeat themselves? Why do teachers repeat themselves? Why do parents repeat themselves? Why has my wife

---

93 Philippians 3:1, New International Version

repeated the admonition to put the lid back on the toothpaste for 42 years? She has even resolved to buy the kind of toothpaste that has the lid attached so it flips, but I still find it terribly hard to put that back in its place. It requires an extra step in the morning—and I'm a busy man with much on my mind. She thinks I do it on purpose. I don't. I'm just occupied with all of the world's burdens, and I'm praying. I'm so overwhelmed that she has to say it over and over and over again until one day maybe I will get it.

Yes, I just moved my tongue toward my cheek.

Repetition, though usually annoying, is an effective teaching and learning tool. He has been telling the believers at Philippi to make the choice to rejoice over and over again. In doing so, he has also been reminding himself.

I think the takeaway here is that choosing joy in tough circumstances is not an automatic or "reflex" response. It must be a deliberate thing. This is not going to be our go-to position when we're facing unfavorable circumstances. We have to consciously choose it. Let's look at a few ways we can make this great choice.

Make the choice to rejoice by identifying and resisting joy killers.

Sin is a killjoy. Remember when David confessed his sin in Psalm 51? One of the things he said was, *"Restore to me the joy of your salvation."*[94] He had lost his joy. When we mess up, we do too.

---

[94] Psalm 51:12, New International Version

Paul mentions certain kinds of people who have a joy-busting agenda. He is talking contextually here about particular individuals. He says it this way: *"Watch out for those dogs, those evildoers, those mutilators of the flesh."*[95] It's like he is posting a big sign that says, "BEWARE OF DOGS." Only in this case, the "dogs" are human beings.

What's this about? Let's give some context. I'm going to tell you the particular joy killer Paul himself had to learn how to resist, one that was becoming a very real problem to the Philippian Christians. This is not the same joy killer most of us (if any of us) will ever have to deal with in our lives, but the principle is the same. The names change, the culture changes, the dynamics change, but there are always going to be people in our life-sphere who seem to thrive on dragging us down. Certainly the Devil can be involved in this. If you're not careful, they can kill your joy. You have to resist them. I mean, we're all going to have to deal with it.

The historic story of redemption and salvation begins back in the early pages of the Bible after the fall into sin. It involves a series of promises and covenants made to individuals who become a nation. That nation is Israel. There are actually 631 specific commandments in the Old Testament. You get all these laws and rules that sort of make up the body of truth of what it means to live an upright life. And it all flows down to us through the Jewish people. The plan was for them to be the delivery mechanism that would eventually bring God's grace and mercy and love to the whole world, embodied in Jesus who comes on the scene as the

---

[95] Philippians 3:2, New International Version

Jewish Messiah (the word *Christ*, the Anointed One, is a messianic term), but also as the Savior of the world.

In the book of Acts, as Christ prepared to ascend back to heaven several weeks after the cross and resurrection, He told his disciples: "Be witnesses in Jerusalem, Judea (Jewish people), Samaria (partly Jewish people but not all), to the uttermost part of the earth (all the nations)." He said, *"make disciples of all nations."* The word *nations* comes from the Greek word *ethnos*, which doesn't mean geographical borders, it means people groups.[96]

Every people group needs to hear about the gospel and be invited into this wonderful relationship that was delivered to us through the great covenants and promises made to the nation of Israel. The early Christians were predominantly Jewish. On the day of Pentecost when the Holy Spirit was poured out, there were Jewish people present who lived throughout the Roman world, having traveled to Jerusalem for a great celebration. Gospel witness started there. The plan wasn't for it to stay there.

Paul says in Romans, *"For I am not ashamed of the gospel of Christ: for it is the power of God to salvation for everyone who believes, for the Jew first and also for the Greek* [or the Gentile]. *"*[97] What is he saying? He is not saying Jewish people get it first. He says they *got* it first. Then it started to spread out. Peter had the keys to the kingdom—given to him by Jesus.[98]

---

[96] See Acts 1:8 & Matthew 28:18-20, New International Version

[97] Romans 1:16, New International Version

[98] See: Matthew 16:18-19

What does a key do? It opens the door. So, Peter opens a door on the Day of Pentecost. Then later, he opens a door to the Gentiles.[99] Soon, Paul is raised up to be a special emissary to the Gentiles. But sadly, there were many Jewish converts—some of them may have been "pseudo-converts"—who insisted that Gentiles become more "Jewish" in order to be accepted. Paul refers to them as Judaizers. They opposed Paul's work among the Gentiles.

Possibly, some of it was personal. After all, Paul had been one of them. Paul was in the Sanhedrin. He was a young man in a hurry, making a name for himself persecuting Christians. Then he had his encounter with Jesus. I can imagine that certain people saw Paul as a traitor. Even Simon Peter had some difficultly fully understanding and accepting Paul's role and his passion.[100]

It was like the Judaizers were saying, "Okay, now we understand the gospel is for the Gentiles. Anybody can be saved, but you can't reject everything about our national heritage." So they insisted, "In order for you to really be truly saved, you have to sort of come and be a little Jewish first, and then you get saved."

The mark of that Judaism was circumcision, which was a mandate given to Abraham—a sign of the covenant God had made to Israel. Circumcision is now a very commonplace thing for male babies, but there was a time when it wasn't. It was then a uniquely Jewish thing. It doesn't have that same meaning to us now. But back then, some were saying, "If you're truly saved, even if you've professed

---

99 See: Acts chapter 10

100 See: Galatians 2:11-14

Jesus by faith, even if you've been baptized, you still have to become a little bit Jewish."

In other words, there was a Jewish "hoop" they insisted Gentiles must jump through. Paul disagreed and conflict ensued. Bitter conflict, at times.

Now, I want to say this so clearly and so unambiguously that you don't misunderstand. Much of the opposition to early Christians came from Jewish people, Jewish structures, and even Christians who were holding onto Jewish traditions. This should in no way ever be interpreted or applied (certainly in any way modern) to indicate a basis for any form of anti-Semitism. That's not what it's about. It's about ideas.

In fact, if you really love and know the history of the Bible, love God, and love God's program, there should be no group of people we have greater respect for and regard for in history, and today, than the Jewish people. I mean that with all my heart. Anti-Semitism, in fact, any kind of racist bigotry—is sinful. Period.

Of course, we say Jesus is their Messiah. Many of them say he is not, and that is a matter of disagreement. But it must never be an excuse for hate or prejudice. God loves all people—and all people groups. So should we.

Do we create "hoops" in our day for some to jump through to become one of "us?" Sure we do. I've never seen a *Christianity Today* profile, "A church in Fairfax, Virginia, is having a big discussion right now because some of the members believe all the men should be circumcised." I mean, I don't think you can grow a church that way, for one thing. "Come on in. We'll cut you up."

But there are some groups and some teachings that add things to the simple Gospel. Maybe it's baptism, or maybe it's some other ritual or work—things that may very well have their place in our lives, but never as a condition for God's grace in saving us.

What is legalism? Legalism is trying to earn righteousness via works. That was what Paul was talking about, when he said, "Beware of dogs." Next to pigs, they were the most unclean of animals in the Old Testament. There is nothing good ever said about a dog in the Bible. Sorry.

Cats aren't mentioned, so we're just going to leave that as an open question.

In fact, in the book of Revelation, it talks about people not in heaven outside of the gates. They're dogs. He is talking about people who want to devour our joy.

In the Book of Galatians, Paul expands on this:

"Mark my words! I, Paul, tell you that if you let yourselves be circumcised, Christ will be of no value to you at all. Again, I declare to every man who lets himself be circumcised that he is obligated to obey the whole law. You who are trying to be justified by the law have been alienated from Christ; you have fallen away from grace. For through the Spirit we eagerly await by faith the righteousness for which we hope. For in Christ Jesus neither circumcision nor uncircumcision has any value. The only thing that counts is faith expressing itself through love."

And:

"Brothers and sisters, if I am still preaching circumcision, why am I still being persecuted? In that case the offense of the cross has been abolished. As for those agitators, I wish they would go the whole way and emasculate themselves!"[101]

Paul was so upset with the agitators, he suggested pretty drastic measures. Yikes!

You say, "Well, nobody wants to do that now." But there are people who will try to say, "In order for you to be saved, you have to have this external stuff." Then also after you get saved, there are people who say you have to have all these rules. Legalism is rules without relationships. Have you ever met Christians who had more rules than Jesus? They're modern day mutilators.

They're also joy-killers.

The joy-killing rules change from generation to generation. There are all kinds of different rules about what it means to look like a Christian and to act like a Christian. "Christians go *here*. Christians go *there*. They don't go *here*. They don't go *there*." Read Romans, chapters thirteen and fourteen. Don't flaunt liberty, don't drag anybody down, and don't be boastful about it, but if there's something you believe is okay for you to do and there's nothing biblically against it, and you know a few Christians might mind, just do it. Have privacy. Exercise your privilege and freedom in privacy.

By the way, there are some things you might not be able to do now but you'll be able to do later. There are some Christians who have

---

[101] Galatians 5:2-6, 12

been delivered from alcoholism, so to even go into a restaurant that serves alcohol is a strong temptation for them. That's a wise thing. If you're with somebody like that, you might not want to take them to that restaurant to flaunt your liberty. It may be that they'll get strong enough in ten years that they'll be able to go to that restaurant. Has God changed his mind? No. There are differences related to where you are in your life with God. We have to think these things through.

When Paul wrote a letter to the Christians at Colossae, he expanded on the idea of trying to be righteous through rules, regulations, and rituals.

"Since you died with Christ to the elemental spiritual forces of this world, why, as though you still belonged to the world, do you submit to its rule? 'Do not handle! Do not taste! Do not touch!'? These rules, which have to do with things that are all destined to perish with use, are based on merely human commands and teachings. Such regulations indeed have an appearance of wisdom, with their self-imposed worship their false humility and their harsh treatment of the body, but they lack any value in restraining sensual indulgence."[102]

Rules don't work. Only a real relationship with the Lord works.

All the time.

---

[102] Colossians 2:20-23, New International Version

Choose joy through authentic worship.

Back when I was a kid growing up, the big measure in the IFB[103] youth group movement was how long your hair was. See, if you had long hair, you were a hippie. My hair came down on my ears a little bit. My dad said, "You're looking like a hippie." "I've seen hippies. I don't look anything like a hippie. I'm nothing like a hippie!"

I went to Bible college. You had to have what they called a "Bill Dowell special" haircut. You had to have a nice gap above the ears, like a military haircut. When we attended a weekly chapel service in the field house, they'd have people at the doors checking our hair as we came in. There's nothing in the Bible about that.

Legalism is actually the enemy of authentic worship.

Paul reminded them and us that, *"we are the circumcision, we who serve God by his Spirit, who boast in Christ Jesus, and who put no confidence in the flesh."*[104]

So true worship is worshiping in the Spirit, true worship is boasting about Jesus, and true worship is not having any confidence in your human nature, trusting God.

Choose joy through heavenly accounting.

When I was first married, my brothers-in-law, my father-in-law, and I went out and played golf. My father-in-law could not play

---

[103] Independent Fundamental Baptist
[104] Philippians 3:3, New International Version

golf at all. He couldn't hit the ball. He was usually off by himself someplace, usually in the woods. We played along. When we finished, I asked him how he did. He replied, "Well, I didn't keep score, but I only lost eleven balls."

That's one way to keep score.

Listen to what Paul said, *"though I myself have reasons for such confidence. If someone else thinks they have reasons to put confidence in the flesh, I have more."* He is basically saying, "You think you're religious? Listen to my record. I was *"circumcised on the eighth day."*

Do you know why they did it on the eighth day? Because when a baby is born, it takes about seven to eight days for the K element in the blood (the coagulating element) to be strong enough. So on the eighth day, the baby can heal more quickly.

He says, *"of the people of Israel."* This is his pedigree, his bona fides. *"of the tribe of Benjamin, a Hebrew of Hebrews."* He even spoke Hebrew. In fact, *"in regard to the law, a Pharisee."* There were only about 6,000 Pharisees in the Jewish world, at the time. "You talk about passion and zeal? I persecuted the church," which was a plus. They sent him out to do that. "As far as right living according to the law, I was faultless." He was a good man, but here's what he says.

"But whatever were gains to me I now consider loss for the sake of Christ." He kept score differently after he got saved. *"What is more, I consider everything a loss because of the surpassing worth of knowing Christ Jesus my Lord, for whose sake I have lost all things. I consider them garbage, that I may gain Christ and be*

found in him, not having a righteousness of my own that comes from the law, but that which is through faith in Christ—the righteousness that comes from God on the basis of faith."[105]

Now go back to that word *garbage* for a moment. That's how it's translated in the New International Version. In the King James, it's translated *dung*, thus the title of this chapter. It means excrement. You could translate it manure.

Maybe I should have titled this chapter, *Canines and Crap*.

Paul is saying, "Everything I thought was important to me to impress God I now consider just a bunch of religious crap based on my pride. I want to know Jesus. I want to know Jesus!"

The issues are different in the twenty-first century than they were in the first century. Like I said, we don't battle over circumcision, but are there things we think are really essential? Are there things you strive for in your life to impress others and maybe thinking to impress God that at the end of the day have nothing to do with spiritual growth and knowing Jesus?

We have to get rid of the baggage and cargo in our lives. Even the religious baggage. Be authentic. I know some Christians who will be more bothered by my use of the word "crap" than about their own self-righteous pride.

---

[105] Philippians 3:4-9, New International Version

Choose joy through a transcendent preoccupation.

What does that mean? Something that's over and above. What's our ultimate magnificent obsession? *"I want to know Christ—yes, to know the power of his resurrection and participation in his sufferings, becoming like him in his death..."* I want to know Christ.[106]

When I was growing up, I had this ongoing debate with my grandfather about who would win in a boxing match in their prime: Cassius Clay (Muhammad Ali) or Joe Louis, who was from Detroit. My grandfather was a big Joe Louis fan. They have a big statue of his fist in Detroit. We'd go around and around about that. So, I started reading about Joe Louis. I devoured many books about him and boxing. I can still tell you everything about Joe Louis's career today. I can tell you how he fought Max Baer and Buddy Baer. I can tell you how he fought a guy named Arturo Godoy, Tami Mauriello (names you've never heard of), Billy Conn (in '41, thirteen rounds and in '46, eight rounds), Jersey Joe Walcott (several fights), and James J. Braddock. I can talk about his "Bum of the Month Club." I know an awful lot about Joe Louis, but I never met the guy.

I didn't really know him.

You can know an awful lot about Christianity, faith, Jesus, but do you know him first as your Lord and Savior, and do you want to know him better?

---

[106] Philippians 3:10, New International Version

When Karen and I first got married, we thought we knew each other. We did up to that point. Now, we've been married 42 years. We know each other a lot better because we've shared a life of experiences. That's how you learn. That's how you get to know somebody. You share life with them, right? Not just sitting around. You share life, all those experiences.

Long before the movie *Titanic* came out (1997), I was fascinated with the story. So as the big movie rolled out, there were several documentaries on television around the same time. One night Karen and I were watching one such program. It told the story of Mr. and Mrs. Straus. They were an old couple who stayed on the ship. Mr. Straus was the founder of Macy's department store, a very wealthy man. He tried to get his wife into a lifeboat, and she wouldn't go. It's a pretty moving story. Mrs. Straus reportedly said something like, "Old man, I have been with you all these years in life. I shall be with you in death."

Powerful.

Just then, Karen reached over and touched my hand. Very cool. She said, "If that ever happens to us, I'm getting in that boat."

How's that for a shared experience?

"I want to know Christ—yes, to know the power of his resurrection and participation in his sufferings, becoming like him in his death."[107]

---

[107] Philippians 3:10, New International Version

How do you grow in intimacy with Jesus? Share His experiences. Paul mentions three.

Share the power of his resurrection.

What's the greatest power on earth? Atom power? Nuclear? Nope.

Resurrection power.

That's the power of the Spirit of God. The same power that brought Jesus back from the dead is in us through the Holy Spirit, and we can tap into that if we know how. The key is faith. And the more we experience resurrection power, the better we get to know Him.

Participate in his sufferings.

What does this mean? Watch the language. When we suffer or feel pain, we may want to invite Him in—and that's a good idea. But Paul says, we need to share in His sufferings. What that does is give us a perspective. It's like the old Arab proverb, "I cried because I had no shoes until I met a man who had no feet."

Hebrews 12:3: *"For consider him that endured such contradiction of sinners against himself, lest you be wearied and faint in your minds."* When you're in pain, don't focus on your pain. Invite him in, but focus on *his* pain. Read about the cross.

Be made conformable to his death.

Death is a surrender. *"Father, into thy hands I commend my spirit,"* Jesus said. He gave up the ghost. That's ultimate surrender. Maybe you know the verse Galatians 2:20. It's a great verse. You ought to know it. Paul says, *"I am crucified with Christ: nevertheless I live; yet not I, but Christ liveth in me: and the life which I now live in the flesh I live by the faith of the Son of God, who loved me, and gave himself for me."*

Right smack dab in the middle of that verse are four words and one punctuation mark that explain everything you need to know about living for God. *"I am crucified with Christ: nevertheless I live; yet not I, but Christ liveth in me..."*.

Those four words and that one comma can change your life.

At every turn, every decision, every choice, every problem, every challenge is a chance for you to be conformed to his death by saying, *"...not I, but Christ..."*

John the Baptist expressed it this way: *"He must increase, but I must decrease."*[108] Jesus said, *"...not my will, but thine, be done."*[109]

Not I, but Christ. The ultimate act of surrender. That's the Christian life, no matter what the barking dogs of legalistic religion say.

---

108 John 3:30, King James Version

109 Matthew 26:39, King James Version

Dogs and dung.

Beware of anybody who adds anything to the pure grace of God through faith. Beware of anybody who over-regulates the Christian life beyond what the Bible teaches. If you're relying on your religious résumé to impress other people and yourself, realize it does not impress God. Beware of dogs. Get rid of the dung. Get it out of your life, and make the choice to rejoice—no matter what.

Think on These Things

Has anyone ever neutralized your joy?

Have you ever been a joy-killer?

What are some present-day "hoops?"

How does legalism defeat true spirituality?

READING:
Philippians 3:1-10
Galatians 2:11-14
Colossians 2:20-23

CHAPTER EIGHTEEN

Are We There Yet?

The famous linguist Yogi Berra, also remembered as an All-Star catcher for the New York Yankees, had a lot of sayings. For example, "You can observe a lot by *watching.*"

People *are* watching. They're watching us. Jesus reminded the disciples that the world would know we were authentic disciples of his by our love for one another. Not by our doctrinal statement (though that's important), not by the stand we take on an issue (that may be important), but by how we treat each other.

Interesting.

Convicting.

The Apostle Peter in his writings reminded us that we always need to be ready to be a witness.[110] Some of the greatest opportunities for witness do not come from the "cold call" for Jesus, but when

---

110 See: 1 Peter 3:15

people come to us with a question. He says be ready to give an answer to anyone who approaches you wanting to know about the hope that is within you. In other words, these are people who see you responding to trouble, crisis, negative experiences, but you're not doing it in a pessimistic way.

You have authentic hope.

Hope is a close relative to joy. How do they know we have hope? It has to be articulated. They know you have hope because you handle stress with joy. In moments that invite all kinds of other choices, you choose joy. You are rejoicing in the Lord. Your entire visage is not *overwhelmed* by circumstances but *transcending* those circumstances because you've made the choice to rejoice.

That's what the book of Philippians is about.

"Not that I have already obtained all this, or have already arrived at my goal, but I press on to take hold of that for which Christ Jesus took hold of me. I press on to take hold of that for which Christ Jesus took hold of me."[111] *In another translation, it says, "...I may apprehend that for which also I am apprehended of Christ Jesus."* The word *apprehend* means to seize. It's like being arrested.

In Paul's case, that's exactly how his great life change came about. He was on the road to Damascus going one direction, breathing out threats and slaughter against Christians. He had an encounter with Jesus on the Damascus road. He was apprehended. He was arrested by Jesus. Instead of chasing followers of Jesus, he started chasing Jesus and chasing people *for* Jesus the rest of his life. He

---

[111] Philippians 3:12, New International Version

was saying, "I was taken hold of. Christ took me over. He seized me. I was apprehended. My life goal is to apprehend the reason he saved me. I want to grow into this salvation. I want to fulfill the reason he saved me."

Why does God save us? What is salvation about? Is it only about us being in heaven one day?

Well, yes, there is a heaven. We're going there in Christ. But that's not the purpose of salvation. It's one of the great blessings and benefits. There are two primary purposes identified in the New Testament. The first is found in Paul's Epistle to the Romans, where it says God has done all this that we might be brought into conformity with Jesus Christ. He has saved us so he can recreate Christ in us, turn us into people like Christ so we can be not only in heaven with him, but also progressively increasingly walking on the earth as models of what Jesus can do in a life.[112]

The second purpose of salvation is highlighted in Paul's letter to the Ephesians.

"For by grace are you saved through faith; and that not of yourselves: it is the gift of God: Not of works, lest any man should boast." For we are his workmanship, created in Christ Jesus unto good works."[113]

We're saved so he can make us like Jesus so we can also do some good works in this world. Good works are not how you get saved, but they're a big part of the equation. Good works are not the *root*

---

112 See: Romans 8:28-30

113 Ephesians 2:8-10, New King James Version

of our salvation, but they are to be the *fruit* of our salvation. Good works are not the *cause* of our salvation, but they certainly should be the *effect* of our salvation.

Choose joy by embracing God's work in progress in us.

Maybe you've seen the bumper sticker or heard the saying, "Be patient; God is not finished with me yet." We are all works in progress. Paul said, "I have not arrived."

There have been many great people who have made their mark on the world and their times. Certainly, the greatest of all would be our Lord Jesus Christ. Next to Jesus Christ, the greatest Christian who walked on the earth was the apostle Paul. That's a no-brainer.

I mean, this guy was sold out. He was all in. At the end of his life, he said, *"I have fought a good fight, I have finished my course, and I have kept the faith."*[114] He did it all. He was a church planter. He was an evangelist. He was a mentor. He was beaten. He was persecuted and left for dead. All the while, he kept going forward. He was a great example of what it means to be a soldier of the cross.

We're talking about growth toward glory. Glory is the ultimate goal. Growth is the dynamic. Have you become complacent in your spiritual life? Do you think you've reached the place where you've arrived and you're on autopilot? Don't ever be satisfied with that.

We talk about contentment and say things like we should be content with what we have. I remind you, in the Scripture we're told to be content with material things. We're never to be covetous

---

[114] II Timothy 4:7, King James Version

people, always clawing and scratching for more. That's lust. That's covetousness. **But we should never be content with what we are.** There should always be part of us that remains restless and eager to grow.

Ted Williams was still taking batting practice when he was 40 years of age, because he wanted to be a better hitter. He hadn't arrived. That's what the great ones do. As a Christian, get rid of the notion that you can reach a level of "maintenance" living. If the apostle Paul was conscious of the fact that he wasn't there yet, neither are we.

The answer to that annoying question from the backseat of every car on every road trip, "Are we there yet?" is no. You can ask it a hundred times, but the answer is no. What he is talking about was embracing that work in progress. I mean, it *is* going to be finished. Remember verse six of the first chapter of Philippians? *"he which hath begun a good work in you will perform it until the day of Jesus Christ."*

What God starts, he finishes. We're not finished yet. We have a long way to go. You may be a young believer. You may be a new believer. You may be a person who has been around for a while, or you may be at the entry-level of spiritual life. By the way, chronology and the simple passage of time do not automatically mean growth.

I know a lot of Christians who have been saved for only two or three years who are much more mature than twenty-year church members. Some have, sadly, never grown.

I remember when I first came to the church I've been shepherding for twenty years. I would have conversations with long-time members that went something like this. They would ask, "Doesn't it say somewhere in the Bible that?" And I would reply, "Well, why don't you know that? You've been coming to this church for that whole period of time. Why don't you know this?" I was probably being annoying, but at some point, believers need to take responsibility and learn basic principles.

My mother used to feed me when I was a baby. But I eventually learned how to feed myself.

Choose joy by cultivating sanctified amnesia.

I heard a story about an old preacher (come to think of it, he was about my current age—yikes). He was preaching and he forgot the words of the song "Amazing Grace." He said, "Now I'm going to tell you, brothers and sisters, it's like that old song, 'Amazing grace, how sweet the sound that saved a wretch like me.' (Awkward pause) 'Oh yes, I love that amazing grace."

Many years ago I was preaching in New York City at a famous church that was started more than a decade before the Civil War. I preached the whole sermon placing Abraham at the burning bush. When I was done, one of my sweet daughters said, "Daddy, wasn't it Moses who was by that burning bush?" She could have held up something that said, "Moses" and it would have helped me, but she just laughed at me and thought it was funny. Whatever.

What is sanctified amnesia? Well, it's a process of deliberately forgetting parts of the past that might hinder our present and future.

"But one thing I do: Forgetting what is behind and straining toward what is ahead."[115]

We have to have a relationship with the past, but we should never live there. There are many things in the past that can paralyze us in the present. We have to put the past behind us in a couple of ways.

Past hurt.

Past failure.

Past success.

The last one in that list may surprise you.

When you rest on a past success, it can get in the way of right now. We can be inspired by certain things, but we shouldn't be paralyzed by anything from the past—be it the distant past, or recent experiences.

Choose joy by keeping your eyes on the prize.

Paul then wrote: *"I press on toward the goal to win the prize for which God has called me heavenward in Christ Jesus."*[116] In other

---

[115] Philippians 3:13, New International Version

[116] Philippians 3:14, New International Version

words, "I am focused this way. I'm not looking back. I am focused this way on the goal."

What is the goal? Heaven? No, but it's in heaven. It's a heavenward goal, but the prize, the goal, is not heaven. It's something else that happens there. I believe it speaks to specific rewards we're going to get based on our service. That's why there's something called the judgment seat of Christ.[117]

It's not a judgment to determine whether you're saved or lost; it's to determine what you've done for Jesus with your life. The Bible talks in the book of Revelation about the heavenly scene and God rewarding people. He gives crowns to them, things that honor and acknowledge the work they've done. So, we're to press forward.

Choose joy by getting a heavenly head start.

"Only let us live up to what we have already attained. Join together in following my example, brothers and sisters, and just as you have us as a model, keep your eyes on those who live as we do. For, as I have often told you before and now tell you again even with tears, many live as enemies of the cross of Christ. Their destiny is destruction, their god is their stomach, and their glory is in their shame. Their mind is set on earthly things. But our citizenship is in heaven. And we eagerly await a Savior from there, the Lord Jesus Christ, who, by the power that enables him to bring everything under his control, will transform our lowly bodies so that they will be like his glorious body."[118]

---

117 See: II Corinthians 5:10

118 Philippians 3:20-21, New International Version

As I mentioned earlier, Philippi was a Roman colony.

When Paul talked about citizenship, it resonated with the Philippians because they related it to Roman citizenship.

Did you ever think of the church as a colony? All of us who are saved have our citizenship in heaven, and we've been left here to colonize this area of the world and spread the gospel and build this colony of believers. That's exactly what Paul was saying.

It doesn't say our citizenship *will be* in heaven when we get there. That may be our future address, but our citizenship is *already* there. I'm a citizen of the United States of America, wherever in the world I may travel or even choose to live. All of us who are saved are citizens of heaven, and I'm going to tell you that should be of foremost importance. We always need to be thinking of how it's done back home. What are they doing back home? Well, they worship, they serve, and they praise. Get a little head start on heaven on earth.

We're eagerly waiting for Jesus. He is going to come and transform us. That's the glory part.

Ultimate transformation.

So why not get a head start? The word for *change* (transform) is the word from which we get our English word *metamorphosis*. When Jesus went up to the mountain with Peter, James, and John, as recorded in Matthew 17, His face changed, and it became radiant. He was transfigured. That's the same Greek word. When it says in Romans 12:2, *"Be not conformed to the world, but be transformed by the renewing of your mind that you may prove what is the good, acceptable, and perfect will of God,"* it's also the same Greek word. And it pops up again elsewhere:

"And we all, who with unveiled faces contemplate the Lord's glory, are being transformed into his image with ever-increasing glory, which comes from the Lord, who is the Spirit."[119]

One day we'll be totally transformed. The prefix in the word metamorphosis, is meta, which means above and beyond. It's also the beginning of our word *metabolism*. Are you familiar with metabolism? Metabolism means there are some people who can eat the exact same thing I eat and never become overweight. They're hard to love.

Metabolism is how you process stuff. It's not a stretch to say one of the things we need to do as we wait for Jesus is to let this spiritual metabolism start working.

Now how do we do that? We have to give it something to work with: the renewing of your mind, the Word of God. That's why we should internalize Scripture. Hide the Word in your heart. It will make a great difference in you across the board.

Isn't this world a wicked place? One day we're going to get to heaven, and it's all going to be wonderful, isn't it? So, why don't we get a head start? We have resurrection power. We have heavenly citizenship. Why don't we decide, "I'm not going to live like the rest of the world lives—depressed, defeated, down in the dumps, negative, and critical. I'm going to have the joy of the Lord. I'm going to make the choice to rejoice. I am going to take that

---

[119] II Corinthians 3:18, New International Version

power, and I'm going to live a little heaven on earth. My home is going to be a heavenly enclave. My church is going to be a place where I have a little touch of heaven because I'm with the people I'm going to spend all eternity with."

Glory is the goal; growth is the process. The great question is: Are you growing?

If you're spiritually healthy, you will grow. People often ask me, "What's your philosophy of church growth?" It's not numbers, because there are things you can do as a pastor and as a church to recruit numbers. You can just get all the unhappy people from other churches. No. I want to be a pastor of a church filled with people who are growing, because God will take care of all the rest.

Are you growing? Are you in the same place spiritually now you were six months ago? That's not the plan of God for your life. He wants you to continue to press on.

Think on These Things

Have you ever been arrested by God?

What are good works, and what part should they play in our lives?

What does it mean to be content?

In what sense should we NEVER be content?

READING:
Philippians 3:12-21
Ephesians 2:1-10
Romans 8:28-30

CHAPTER NINETEEN

It Just Takes Two

There's a phrase that appears many times in Scripture, particularly the New Testament. It's an archaic way of saying that word got around. "It was noised about." We hear that many times of Jesus. That was basically how people found out stuff 2,000 years ago in a pre-technological age. No *Twitter*, no Internet, no texting, no radio. Just interpersonal communication.

They talked.

Word was getting around that Epaphroditus, who had left the church at Philippi and traveled more than 600 miles to the city of Rome in order to encourage the apostle Paul, had returned. The church at Philippi had raised some funds to help with his imprisonment. We don't know how many people were in the church. It had been a while since the church was established. We learned about that in the Book of Acts.[120] The Philippian jailer and

---

120 See: Acts 16:13-40

his family, Lydia, and others were saved. There were certainly many more, including Epaphroditus.

They were meeting in homes or in makeshift places, sometimes rented halls, as was the case with Tyrannus' hall in Ephesus. We don't know where they met, but the word got around. "We're going to have a meeting. Epaphroditus is back. He's bringing a report of his trip to Rome, and he's going to bring some special message."

They gathered.

Maybe they had a time of prayer and worship, and then Epaphroditus was front and center. He began to read from a scroll. It was a letter—a very intimate letter—from Paul. They had sent Epaphroditus to be an encouragement to Paul, and Paul is writing back all of these wonderful profundities filled with encouragement.

How exciting!

Epaphroditus read to them, "Don't worry. The Lord who has begun a good work in you will be faithful to complete it until the day of Jesus Christ." He said, "For me to live is Christ and to die is gain. I want Christ to be magnified in my body, whether by life or by death." He talked a little about getting along with each other. "Let nothing be done through strife or vainglory." They may have looked at each other and said, "What has he heard?"

Then the scene shifted into this grand discussion of Jesus, our ultimate example, "Who, being in the form of God, thought it not robbery to be equal with God, humbled himself, became of no reputation, was obedient unto death, even the death of the cross.

God has highly exalted him and given him a name which is above every name."

They're listening intently.

Then they learned about Timothy and how he was doing. Then Epaphroditus read about himself, about the illness they had heard about, that he had been sick, even close to death. The people were so glad to see him in good health, this risk-taker, this man who was all in, who had gone and had now returned.

They heard about Paul's religious résumé and how everything he had ever done religiously had been a waste of time, because the main thing was to know Jesus and the power of his resurrection and the fellowship of his sufferings.

They're filled with joy, hearing the Word from this authoritative apostle.

Then...

"I plead with Euodia and I plead with Syntyche to be of the same mind in the Lord. Yes, and I ask you, my true companion, help these women since they have contended at my side in the cause of the gospel, along with Clement and the rest of my co-workers, whose names are in the book of life. Rejoice in the Lord always. I will say it again: Rejoice! Let your gentleness be evident to all. The Lord is near."[121]

---

[121] Philippians 4:2-5, New International Version

Can you imagine how this changed the mood—and the wonderful moment?

It was clear that two people in the church were having a hard time getting along.

Maybe some people looked at the women—who were undoubtedly not sitting together. Whatever the basis for their "feud," by that time many had chosen sides. It was "Team Euodia" or "Team Syntyche." We don't know what the nature of the disagreement was. We can ascertain pretty correctly, I think, that it wasn't a big deal. It wasn't doctrinal. No one was spreading false doctrine. Nothing like that.

But they had a strong disagreement that had polarized and paralyzed the church.

These two ladies are forever linked in Biblical infamy. Just two to tan*gle*. That's all it takes to get bad attitudes, for the Devil to find a way in. He's talking to a local church, a community, a family. "They need to agree in the Lord. Epaphroditus, you help them and involve some of the others, because we're all in the Book of Life," he says.

Making the choice to rejoice becomes difficult when we are part of, or even near conflict. How can we resolve things?

Move conflict to common ground.

We're never going to find complete agreement on every issue of life between any two people. Never. So we have to move any potential conflict to common ground. What does he say? "They need to learn to agree with each other in the Lord."

In the Lord.

What does it mean? It could mean a common goal—the work of the Lord. It could mean that God is watching always. What it isn't is just a little suffix you put at the end of something, like they do in some places where they say, "Oh, she's sure ugly, bless her heart." You think by saying, "Bless her heart" it sanctifies everything. "He can't preach, bless his heart. But he's sure sincere, bless his heart." "Well, I don't like her, but I love her in the Lord." No. You can't get away with that. "In a theological sense I love that person." What? No.

"In the Lord" means you're managing that dynamic in light of the bigger picture, in light of the bigger relationship. Agreeing in the Lord means to agree in *the things of the Lord.* We are called upon by God to have 100 percent agreement in the things of the Lord, but it doesn't mean we're going to agree on everything.

I have a lot of opinions, and you have a lot of opinions. We may not agree in politics and in the voting booth.

Some people are vegetarians, others are normal.

You get the point.

What Paul counseled was, "I want these people to agree in the Lord." In other words, find a point of agreement bigger than your area of disagreement. And never let disagreements define you or your relationships.

If you're a Christian and you want to get along with brothers and sisters, define your relationship on those things you hold in common. How about the word *fellowship?* I was raised Baptist. "Yeah, we're going off to church to have some fellowship." That meant we were going to eat some food. Because *fellowship* in the Greek surely had something to do with food. It does not. The Greek word is *koinonia*, and it means sharing in common.

Fellowship means we have certain things in common.

Somebody once said, "If two of us agree on everything, one of us is worthless." Another one said, "If two people agree on everything, you can be sure only one is doing the thinking."[122] We can always find common ground. Does it mean you don't fight for what you believe in? No, you do. But in the church we come together in the Lord.

He says another way you agree is by rejoicing in the Lord always because if you're rejoicing together, you have a really hard time working against each other. Just start rejoicing. When you get with another person, just start rejoicing in the Lord, not in what you disagree on. *"Let your gentleness be evident to all."* The word *gentleness* in the NIV is an interesting word. In the King James it's translated *moderation*. The best English translation is "Let your sweet reasonableness be evident to all." Be a reasonable person. Don't be extreme in your opinions.

We all know extreme people. A fanatic, Winston Churchill famously said, is "someone who cannot change his mind and will not change the subject." The only things worth being fanatical

---

[122] Attributed to Former House Speaker, Sam Rayburn, and Lyndon B. Johnson.

about the things of the Lord. But people get fanatical about so many other things. I see it all time.

On *Facebook.*

"Let your sweet reasonableness be known to all men." What he was saying was, "Ladies, be reasonable. Don't be extreme." Stop using absolutist language. Stop using extreme language. Think about how we appear before the world.

Fight for your convictions, but just choose your preferences.

We all have preferences. Just choose them, have them, but be honest with yourself and others. "This is what I prefer."

Choose joy by praying your way to tranquility.

Prayer works!

If you could just do one thing to change how you feel… "I just feel this way." Pray. *"Do not be anxious about anything, but in every situation, by prayer and petition,"* Have a list, *"with thanksgiving,"* have the right attitude, *"present your requests to God. And the peace of God, which transcends all understanding will guard your hearts and your minds."*[123]

Remember, Paul was chained to a guard even though he was under house arrest. When he used the Greek word for *guard*, he related it to his chain: "Just like this guard is chained to me and always here,

---

[123] Philippians 4:6-7, New International Version

God will be guard your mind so that you won't be filled with worry."

There's nothing in the text about how God will fix the problem. He does not say if you start praying and give your list, God is going to start making things better. That's not how it works. There's no indication he's going to fix anything you're praying about.

Sometimes God says, "Yes." Sometimes he says, "No." Sometimes he says, "Not now." That's the way it works. He answers all prayer.

Prayer does not always change things.

But prayer always changes *us*.

You pray. You give it to God by praying. Your mind changes, and God's peace starts taking over. We need more of that.

Choose joy by thinking on purpose.

I once saw a cartoon that said: "My parents can send me to college, but they can't make me think." There are a lot of people like that, I guess. Do you think on purpose? Do you deliberately think about things or do you sort of let your mind wander like you're in a dream state? When you go to sleep and you're in rapid eye movement and you're dreaming, you're bouncing from here to there or there. You're tall. You're short. You're an elephant. Anything can happen in your dreams.

When you're awake, do you let your mind wander about like that? Do you daydream or do you constantly work on your mind by planting seeds and putting good stuff in it? If you don't put good stuff in it, all of the bad stuff will take over. You'll find it easy to drift toward the negative and cynical. You have to counteract that.

"Finally, brothers and sisters, whatever is true, whatever is noble, whatever is right, whatever is pure, whatever is lovely, whatever is admirable—if anything is excellent or praiseworthy—think about such things."[124]

Deliberately think about the right things. He says, "Whatever is true." If you're feeding and dwelling on something that is not verifiably true, replace it with something that's is. "Whatever is noble." Don't get lost in the petty stuff. Think big thoughts. Make sure it's right, factually correct, right with God, righteous. Make sure it's pure. If you feed on garbage and that's all you think about, you're going to have an impure heart. Think about lovely stuff, something that's admirable, excellent, praiseworthy. Think about such things.

By the way, every one of these qualities happens when you think about God's Word. Put it in your heart. Hide it in your heart. Internalize it.

I was a youth pastor for a long six months before I became a pastor back in 1977.

I challenged the students to memorize one Scripture a week and not change anything else in their study habits and they'd get better grades the next quarter. Why? Because when you put the Word of God in your mind, it expands your mind. It makes wise the simple.

---

[124] Philippians 4:8-9, New International Version

It'll give you greater clarity of thought. It'll give you greater powers of the mind. I believe that's true.

Call it supernatural brain food.

Do you have a big test coming up? Are you going to take the bar exam? Are you going to take the CPA exam? Do you have a big course you're taking? Why don't you start memorizing Scripture? Still study the stuff. "Well, I memorized the Scripture. I didn't have time to study the material, but I thought God would put it into my head." No, you still have to do the work, but internalizing scripture will give you greater recall. I believe that with all my heart.

Not many people memorize scriptures these days, but they know sports scores, batting averages, dialogue from movies and lyrics from favorite songs—yet not scripture. I believe you're missing out on the very thing you need to change how the inside of you feels and thinks to respond to the outside world.

One verse a week. The equivalent of a tweet a week, 140 characters, bite size. Just once a week. How do you seize it? Ask God to show you what to memorize. Hopefully you're starting by reading the Scripture, and God says, "Here's a verse I want to make a reality in your life." Seize it, and then pray it. Turn that verse into a prayer. You're talking to God about the verse. Then say it. Confess with your mouth.

When you speak something out loud, you remember it more easily. Confess with your mouth. The word is *meditate* in the Hebrew language. Joshua 1:8 says, *"This book of the law shall not depart out of your mouth, but you should meditate in it day and night."*

The imagery in the Hebrew language is of a cow chewing the cud.

That's the image God uses in the Old Testament about meditating on Scripture. Bring it back up and chew on it some more. Keep the Word as a preoccupation. It'll make a great difference.

"Whatever you have learned or received or heard from me, or seen in me—put it into practice. And the God of peace will be with you."[125]

We're Book people. Not only do we have the Book of God, but we have the Book of Life. The Book of Life is a record of those who are saved. It's a "Who's Who" of the redeemed.

If you're saved, you're in the book. If you're not saved, you're not in the book yet. You need to get in the register, get in the record, get in God's book. Once you're in God's book, then get into God's Book. Get God's Book in you, and you can live life powerfully and joyfully.

And you'll never have a problem making the choice to rejoice.

---

[125] Philippians 4:9, New International Version

Think on These Things

How does conflict impact a local church?

What should be the focus of our agreement?

How can selfish ambition divide a church?

How are we to be BOOK people?

READING:
Philippians 4:1-9
Acts 16:13-40
Psalm 133

CHAPTER TWENTY

No Matter What

A while back, I was walking through an airport. I don't remember exactly where. A person ran up behind me and said, "Excuse me, sir." I turned, and he asked, "Are you an author?"

I stopped, because obviously he was an intelligent person.

I said, "Well, yes. Yes, I am." It's sort of nice to be noticed. He said, "Are you also a pastor?"

I said, "Correct. Yes, I am."

"Is your name Rick Warren?"

"No. Excuse me, I have a plane to catch."

A few years ago, Rick (the author of *The Purpose Driven Life* and the founding pastor of Saddleback Church) and Kay Warren faced a tragedy that shook the Christian community, as well. Their adult son, who had been wrestling for a long time with mental illness, tragically took his own life. So very sad.

Kay Warren was a breast cancer survivor who had already been through so much. As they were making their way to their son's home, knowing what was awaiting them, she picked up a piece of jewelry. It was a bracelet that she had crafted and engraved with the words, "Choose Joy."

The words were important to her, because after a health battle a year or two earlier, she had written a book about joy. It's called *Choose Joy: Because Happiness Isn't Enough*, and it became a best-seller. She wrote:

"Happiness is completely connected to what's happening to us on the external circumstances of our lives. Joy is unrelated to what's happening to us on the outside. If joy is only tied to our external circumstances we're all lost; very few of us ever experience joy. But when joy is turned around and has my definition of joy—it's the settled assurance that God is in control of all the details of my life, the quiet confidence that ultimately everything is going to be all right, and the determined choice to praise him in all things.

That has nothing to do with what circumstances are happening in my life. It has everything to do with what I believe about God, what I believe he can do on the inside of me, and my choice then in response to what's happening to me is to give praise back to him. That becomes something that's within my control. I can't always control what's happening to me on the outside, but I can most definitely control my response, what I do with it, what I believe about God, what I believe he's going to do about it. So then joy actually becomes something I can attain."[126]

It's so true. It's there. It's available 100 percent of the time, 24/7. There's never a moment in your existence in Christ that you don't have the capacity for joy. There's never a time you can't choose it. By choosing it, you're deliberately activating it by faith.

When you get saved and open your heart to Christ, God implants this well of living water. What does water do? It refreshes. What does water do? It cleanses. What does water do? It is a source of energy. If you know the Lord, you have that well of water in you. It's deep in you. It's implanted in you and part of God's process. But it's not always bubbling up. It's not always flowing up into your life in a particular moment.

That has to be deliberately activated by faith.

So when you choose joy out of obedience, when you say, "Lord, contrary to these circumstances, contrary to how I even feel, I am choosing joy. I am depending upon you and asking you by the power of the Holy Spirit living within me (that well of water) as I make this choice to let me experience joy every single time," you will not only choose joy; you'll experience it.[127]

It's not an automatic thing. Happiness is fleeting. It's dependent upon circumstances. Joy does not depend on circumstances. It works best against and contrary to circumstances, but it's not

---

[126] "Choose Joy: Because Happiness Isn't Enough," by Kay Warren

[127] See: John chapter four

something that happens automatically. We have to make the choice in the troubled moment to choose joy.

Make the choice to rejoice by learning how to be content.

That's a tough one. Learning how to be content.

"I rejoiced greatly in the Lord that at last you renewed your concern for me. Indeed, you were concerned, but you had no opportunity to show it. I am not saying this because I am in need, for I have learned to be content whatever the circumstances. I know what it is to be in need, and I know what it is to have plenty. I have learned the secret of being content in any and every situation, whether well fed or hungry, whether living in plenty or in want. I can do all this through him who gives me strength."[128]

He was talking about contentment. He had a spiritually mature relationship with his circumstances.

"Keep your lives free from the love of money and be content with what you have, because God has said, 'Never will I leave you; never will I forsake you.'"[129]

"But godliness with contentment is great gain. For we brought nothing into the world, and we can take nothing out of it. But if we have food and clothing, we will be content with that."[130]

---

[128] Philippians 4:10-13, New International Version

[129] Hebrew 13:5, New International Version

[130] I Timothy 6:7-8, New International Version

Contentment.

The opposite of *content* is another word that starts with *C.*

Covet.

What does it mean to covet? It means to have a strong desire for something. It's a synonym of lust. Paul said in Romans 7, *"For I would not have known what coveting really was if the law had not said, 'You shall not covet.'"* It's the same thing. Lust is to real desire, what cancer is to a healthy cell. You desire things. *Covet* is beyond that. Coveting becomes a burning desire.

In fact, in every commandment of God (the other nine commandments), coveting is part of those. "You should have no other gods before me, but if you covet the glory, you see." *"Thou shalt not steal."* That's coveting. Committing adultery is coveting. It's all related. Coveting means wanting more.

A synonym for *content* in the Greek and then into the English language would be the word *enough.*

God wants us to be content with our circumstances, with our position, with our possessions. Do you have enough? "Well, not quite. I could use a little bit more." That's covetous. Paul says, *"I have learned."* Why? Because it's not natural. We want more, more, more. God says get rid of the idea of more. Coveting is to have a burning desire.

The Bible says in 1 Timothy anybody who wants to be rich (has a burning desire) is asking for trouble (paraphrase). We should have a burning desire for God, for the things of God, for holiness, and for the power of God, but not a burning desire for the fleeting things of this dying world.

I'm not talking about ambition. There is healthy desire, but when desire turns into frustration because you have a burning desire and somebody else got something you wanted, that means you don't have enough. Someone is always going to have a bigger house than you do. Someone is always going to have a better car than you do. Someone is always going to have a lot of things you don't have. You have what you have. I have what I have. I'm right where I am because this is God's plan for me at this time.

Let me let you in on a life-secret. If you really believe God has more for you, start being content with where you are and what you have and make the best of it. Now, some of you are thinking, "Oh. Okay. Yes, Lord, I'm content (wink, wink) with what I have." The Lord saw you wink even in your heart, so he knows your heart. Be content. Consider enough to be enough.

Make the choice to rejoice by confessing strength through Christ.

We love this verse, don't we?

"I can do all things through Christ who strengthens me."

It doesn't say, "I can do all things!" "I can jump over this building." No, you can't. "I'm a can-do kind of person." Maybe you are, and there's nothing wrong with having a positive mental attitude. But if you have a burning desire to see Washington, DC, and a positive mental attitude that by getting on I-66 and driving west you can get there—you may be sincere, and you may be passionate, but you're going the wrong way. You're never going to get there.

Positive thinking without God is a waste of time.

What's the context? Paul is talking about, "I can handle anything because I have a vital relationship with Jesus Christ, and he strengthens me." Let me shorten it even more. "I got this through Christ." If you're going through a bad patch, "I got this through Christ. It's not in myself, not because I'm brilliant or have skills. I got this because of that powerful relationship."

The world will use the word *affirmation*. It's not my favorite word because it's tied to a bunch of New Age philosophy. I prefer the word, "confess." To confess with your mouth, we say it. Sometimes you have to say that thing out loud. He says, *"I've learned the secret."* Do you like that word? I like that word *secret*. Everybody likes a secret, right?

A few years ago, there was a book that came out called *The Secret*. Oprah and others promoted it. It's about the law of attraction and how the universe will work when you believe a certain thing and through visualization, the law of attraction will start bringing those things to you.

But, I think such thinking is not only un-biblical—it's dangerous. First, I do believe there are spiritual laws of sowing and reaping. That's clear in Scripture, but the problem I have is with the idea that it's the universe helping us. We're not trusting in the universe. In fact, the word *universe* in the Bible is the same word as *world*. It's translated from the Greek word *cosmos*.

When you read about the universe or the world, the world system, it's not always in a positive light. The Apostle John said that the world is controlled by Satan. Jesus said, "Protect them from the world, the universe, the cosmos." I'm not praying for the universe to help me. The universe hates me, and it hates you.[131]

You say, "It seems like the universe is against me." It is, because it's controlled by the devil. You don't want the universe to bless you. You want God Almighty to bless you, and He is far stronger than the universe. "I've learned a secret. I can do all things through Christ." I like how the Amplified Bible explains words in the text. *"I can do all things [which He has called me to do]."* There's a qualifier. I can show up tomorrow at Nationals Park and say, "I'm here to play second base. I can do all things." No, I can't. I can do all things that _He has called me to do_.

It's all about confident dependence on God.

Meta-Economics.

Making a choice to rejoice often involves a "heavenly" kind of economics. Any of you who have studied undergrad or graduate level economics know there are basically two categories of economics that are analyzed. One is called *macroeconomics*, and the other is *microeconomics*.

Macroeconomics is big economics—people who analyze tax policy to see its long-range effect on job creation, or people who study tariffs to see how they're going to impact inflation. There are

---

[131] See: I John 5:19 & John 17:15-19

people who do this. It's not an exact science. A lot of economists disagree. Harry Truman used to say, "I don't like talking to economists. They have too many hands. Because they're always saying, 'On the other hand.'"

Microeconomics is your checkbook. It's your budget. In our marriage, we have a division of labor, of responsibility, and things we focus on. We always have, even when the kids were small. People would say, "What do you handle, and what does your wife?" I'd say, "Well, I handle big things, and she handles little things."

"Well, give us some examples."

"Right now, I'm working on our family's position on peace in the Middle East. Karen is raising the children."

Macro versus *micro*.

The prefix *meta*, in this context, means "way beyond." I want you to think of economics that are beyond macro and micro. They're beyond. They're God's economics. They work the way God works.

He's so meta.

"Yet it was good of you to share in my troubles. Moreover, as you Philippians know, in the early days of your acquaintance with the gospel, when I set out from Macedonia, not one church shared with me in the matter of giving and receiving, except you only; for even when I was in Thessalonica, you sent me aid more than once when I was in need. Not that I desire your gifts; what I desire is that more be credited to your account. I have received full payment and

have more than enough. I am amply supplied, now that I have received from Epaphroditus the gifts you sent. They are a fragrant offering, an acceptable sacrifice, pleasing to God. And my God will meet all your needs according to the riches of his glory in Christ Jesus."[132]

Isn't it interesting that so many of the churches Paul helped hadn't helped him? But this particular church at Philippi was a generous church. "

For even when I was in Thessalonica, you sent me aid more than once when I was in need."

Paul was content. If he didn't get an offering, he just made some tents, because he was a tentmaker.

I love verse 17. I think this is the most important verse in the chapter. It's more important than verse 13 (*"I can do all things through Christ."*). It's more important than verse 19 (*"My God shall supply all your need."*).

"Not that I desire your gifts; what I desire is that more be credited to your account."

Do you know you have an account in heaven if you're a child of God? Did you know there's an account, and every time you serve, every time you give, every time you invest in ministry (your time, your talent, your treasure) you're getting a deposit into that account? God watches. Some of you are trying to max out your

---
[132] Philippians 4:14-19, New International Version

401(k). You're looking at your account. You get a statement of your account.

Paul says, "I don't need your money." Did you ever hear a preacher say that before? Can I tell you something? I don't need your money, and the church I pastor doesn't need your money. God is in charge. He'll supply the needs.

I believe in tithing. Ten percent of your gross income goes first to the Lord. I believe the tithe should go to the local church. The Bible talks about the church being God's house, but people quibble.[133] You think, "Well, you're just saying that so you can get the budget up." I believe if you start being a giving person, you become content and stop being covetous. If you're a covetous person, you're not a giver. You're a taker.

Oil and water.

If you want to really learn how to be content, you have to start giving something away. I'm going to challenge you right now. For the next two months, give a tithe of your money to St. Jude's. I believe it's a worthy cause. If you think that I am a preacher only interested in my ministry budget, give somewhere else. Of course, I believe a tithe is better going to the church, and I believe there are blessings that accompany that, but I'm talking about learning how to be a giver.

Then track and see how God blesses your generosity. This is a life-principle that transcends any budget or any church. "I desire that you give not because I need a gift but because you have an

---

[133] I Timothy 3:15, King James Version

account." Are you a giver or a taker? Are you a receiver? Giving and receiving. We do both.

"I have received full payment and have more than enough. I am amply supplied, now that I have received from Epaphroditus the gifts you sent. They are a fragrant offering, an acceptable sacrifice, pleasing to God. And my God will meet all your needs according to the riches of his glory in Christ Jesus."[134]

He was giving them a receipt.

Now he says before that he talked about God doing these things, supplying our needs, and meeting these needs in a very, very special way. How does he do this? He uses meta-economics. He says, "I have learned these things. I've learned them the hard way. I don't need your money, but God always takes care of me. He does it when you give. It's like a fragrant offering."

The offerings in the Old Testament on the altar in the temple emitted savory aromas. You say, "What? Like perfume?" No. What was being sacrificed? Animals. A picture of the ultimate sacrifice of Jesus to come. God says, "Every time you practice sacrifice, every time you give into somebody else, every time you do a good work, every time." He is talking in the context of meeting his needs. It's something that smells really good to God.

Think really good brisket.

It's something that rises up before him in a way that is fragrant. I'm sure there's much that happens on Planet Earth that smells

---
[134] Philippians 4:18-19, New International Version

horrible to God. I'm sure there's much that happens even among Christians that just stinks to high heaven. But when we function as people who are content, full of Christ, trusting him for our supply, he says, *"And my God will supply all your needs according to His riches in glory in Christ Jesus."*

Riches related to God are talked about several ways in scripture. Let me give you three of them quickly. There are the *riches of his goodness.* The Bible talks about that. Do you know what that is? That means there are things God does because he is God. Whether you hate him or love him, whether you're saved or not, it rains on the just and the unjust. God still blesses and watches over people. That's the riches of his goodness.

Then there are the *riches of his grace.* We find that in another place. What's that? Those are specific riches that come to us in salvation, the riches that come to us because Jesus died as a sacrifice. Here he talks about according to his *riches in glory.* That's God's supernatural provision of our needs.

The source of what we need to serve God, the source of what we need to send missionaries, is not the bank, not the economy, not even flesh and blood. The source is God. He has tremendous supply, and he wants to bless us, watch over us, and use us.

Years ago, I read this story. Back over a century ago, a person wanted to take a transatlantic trip on a major ocean liner from Britain to the United States. The person wasn't a sophisticated traveler. He barely scrounged up enough to buy a ticket. When he got the ticket, he couldn't really read the ticket because he was illiterate.

He found his way to the lowest level of the ship and brought along with him a little bit of bread, a few little things to eat that would last maybe a day, but he had no money left for any food. Before long, the food ran out. He would sneak up to the upper levels, look into the window, and see people all dressed for dinner and eating four- or five-course dinners.

On the last day of the trip as he was preparing to leave the ship he encountered somebody who asked, "We'll be in New York soon. What's the first thing you're going to do?"

"I'm going to try to find something to eat, but I have no money."

"Why are you so hungry?"

"I didn't have any money for food. I've been hungry for the last couple of days."

"Let me see your ticket."

His ticket actually included meals. He had the right to sit at a table every single time food was served and eat meals, but instead, out of his ignorance, he didn't.

Salvation is not just a ticket to get to heaven. It's all-inclusive. It includes meals, clothing, shelter, whatever you need. If you're not receiving that from God, either you just don't know it's yours or you haven't learned there's still one thing you must do to activate that process. You have to become the kind of person who puts God first in what you have so he can give you the rest of what you need.

No matter what.

FINAL THOUGHTS

Would it surprise you if I confessed that I don't always make the choice to rejoice?

Sad.

And dumb.

But true.

Sometimes I actually choose to wallow in negative thoughts and emotions.

It happened while I was writing this book.

It's a struggle.

A battle.

A constant challenge.

But I'm getting better.

And I'm still growing. – **DRS**

Think on These Things

How can we have a mature relationship with our circumstances?

What does it mean to COVET?

What are "meta"-economics?

What is tithing—and why should I practice it?

READING:
Philippians 4:10-19
John 17:15-19
Malachi 3:8-10

ACKNOWLEDGEMENTS

I want to thank Tracey Dowdy, my editorial assistant. Her work on this project was essential to what it has become. She also contributed the foreword—setting the tone for the whole book.

I am also grateful to Rachel Walker and Holly Slater for lending their expert eyes to my sometimes-tortured prose. And to our entire church staff and several others who helped as "beta" readers, I am also deeply indebted.

Eowyn Riggins has created yet another great book cover, and Rachel Green at Penn Oaks Publishing has once again produced a great interior layout.

Christy McGivern has been so helpful with ideas for marketing and distribution.

And the best is yet to come.

Expectation Books—a ministry of Expectation Church in Fairfax, Virginia, is a relatively young endeavor, but we're already seeing fruit and hearing testimonies about how God is using the books.

We'd love to hear from YOU: comments@expectationbooks.com.

This rising tide is starting to lift some boats—to the glory of God!
— **DRS**

ABOUT THE AUTHOR

David R. Stokes is an ordained minister, Wall Street Journal bestselling author, commentator, broadcaster, and columnist. He's been married to the love of his life, Karen, since 1976. They have three daughters and seven grandchildren. And they all live in the great and beautiful Commonwealth of Virginia. He has served as the senior minister at the ministry now known as Expectation Church in Fairfax, Virginia since 1998.

David's website is:
http://www.davidrstokes.com
Follow David on **FACEBOOK**:
https://www.facebook.com/DavidRStokesAuthor/
Follow David on **TWITTER**:
https://twitter.com/DavidRStokes
Follow David on **AMAZON**:
https://amazon.com/author/davidstokes

www.ingramcontent.com/pod-product-compliance
Lightning Source LLC
Chambersburg PA
CBHW031257110426
42743CB00040B/725